GOD

AT THE

KITCHEN TABLE

GOD

AT THE

KITCHEN TABLE

Teaching Your Religious

and Moral Beliefs

to Your Children

SCOTT COOPER

 THREE RIVERS PRESS · NEW YORK

To my parents, Martel and Maurine Cooper,
who gave me a solid foundation while still allowing me
to grow into my own uniqueness.

To Julie, with all my love.

■ ■ ■

Published by Three Rivers Press, New York, New York.
Member of the Crown Publishing Group, a division of Random House, Inc.

www.randomhouse.com

THREE RIVERS PRESS and the Tugboat design are
registered trademarks of Random House, Inc.

Printed in the United States of America

Design by Barbara Sturman

Library of Congress Cataloging-in-Publication Data
Cooper, Scott.
God at the kitchen table : teaching your religious and moral beliefs
to your children / Scott Cooper.—1st ed.
1. Christian education—Home training.   2. Christian education of
children. 3. Moral education (Elementary)   I. Title.
BV1590.C59   2002
291.4'41—dc21   2001045695

ISBN 0-609-80918-0

10 9 8 7 6 5 4 3 2 1

First Edition

ACKNOWLEDGMENTS

Among many other things, George Gallup, Jr., has been head of the Princeton Religion Research Center, headquartered in Princeton, New Jersey, for several years. I'm thankful to Mr. Gallup for his personal attention in answering questions and having his organization provide me with statistical information that I've used in this book. I'd also like to thank Professor Sandra L. Hofferth of the University of Michigan Institute for Social Research for her personal assistance with reviewing other helpful social indicators.

The library staffs of the Graduate Theological Union, the Golden Gate Baptist Theological Seminary, and Sonoma State University, in Northern California, were all very helpful in helping me do research via their facilities. I'm thankful for their assistance.

I'm especially appreciative to my wonderful editor, Betsy Rapoport. Not only is she a talented and skilled professional, she has the personal warmth and people skills that help keep a writer encouraged and on course. I feel fortunate to be associated with her. Thanks also to Stephanie Higgs and Cindy Berman for their kind help.

As usual, I'm deeply appreciative of my wife, Julie, for her significant contribution. She has been invaluable in providing advice on the text. I'll always be thankful for her love and partnership. I'm grateful to Adam, Jackson, and Brooke for being the greatest gifts I could have hoped for and the inspiration for this book.

CONTENTS

Introduction, viii

INTRODUCTION

❧

FOR SEVEN YEARS, MY WIFE AND I WERE UNABLE TO HAVE CHILDREN. We were probed, poked, and tested in ways that I didn't think were humanly possible. Finally, we got to the end of all of our doctors' efforts and were advised that we had a 6 percent chance of ever having children (how they came up with such an exact number, I've never known). It was only a few months after this announcement, however, that our oldest son was conceived. For people who wanted children and had not been able to have them, this was like winning the Lotto. Even more amazing, we won two more Lottos—today we have three wonderful children.

Winning the Lotto three times changed our lives in many ways (just as winning your Lottos has changed yours). Besides the great happiness, joy, and fun our children have brought into our lives, they have brought us more confusion, a deeper appreciation of our own weaknesses, and greater vulnerability to sorrow. Fortunately, they have also forced us to develop greater patience and less self-centeredness. We find ourselves dealing with new issues constantly—especially the issue of what to teach our children so that they can be happy, beneficial, and self-reliant. This led us to the important questions "What should we teach our children about religion and morality, and how should we teach them?"

I had a strong incentive to grapple with these questions. From a fairly young age, I'd been fascinated by religion and philosophy. While I tend to be a private person when it comes to my personal religious beliefs, they are an important part of my life. And though I'm by no means a professional theologian or philosopher, over the years I've spent a fair amount of time reading, thinking, writing, and taking course work relating to the issues of religion, philosophy, and human education and development. I've also had the opportunity, both before and after our children arrived, to be directly involved with youth-development activities through teaching, coaching, and participating on education and drug-prevention boards.

I'm clearly not alone in my interest in religion or in my desire for my children to receive a religious education. According to 1998 Gallup polling data, 87 percent of American adults considered religion to be very important (60 percent) or fairly important (27 percent) in their lives. As of 1998, 82 percent of American adults expressed a desire for spiritual growth in their lives—up from 58 percent in 1994. And during the same year, 89 percent of American adults said they would want a child of theirs to receive religious training.

However, while we know that we want our children to grow up with a strong sense of right and wrong and an anchoring spirituality, we're unclear on how to provide that foundation. We're not sure exactly what our kids learn when we drop them off for formal religious training—or perhaps we want our kids to develop a sense of spirituality beyond an organized religion. We somehow need to integrate the teaching of our values into home lives that are typically overstuffed with careers, carpooling, homework, sports, after-school activities, and more.

I've written *God at the Kitchen Table* to help you provide your kids with the religious and moral training that grows out of both universal values and personal beliefs. The book is in part the outcome of my own family's efforts over the past several years to provide religious and moral education in our home. For us, the kitchen table is the nerve center of the house, where we all meet, relax, and get a chance to really talk. It's inspired a lot of important conversations with our kids. I view a parent's role as loving, protecting, and teaching his or her child. Our institutionalized world has taken over much of the training of our children, and this has generally been positive and supportive. But I remain convinced that, regardless of who actually carries out the teaching itself, we as parents need to ultimately be in charge of overseeing our children's academic and religious training. My hope is that this book will be of help to you in passing on important religious and moral beliefs to your children.

PART ONE

Providing Religious and Moral Training

The Need for Religious and Moral Training

Train up a child in the way he should go: and when he is old,
he will not depart from it.

—PROVERBS 22:6

WHEN I WAS A CHILD, RELIGIOUS LIFE WAS A LOT MORE SIMPLE.
In the "churched" tradition that I grew up in, our Sunday ritual
actually began on Saturday night. After watching *The Jackie Gleason
Show* or *The Red Skelton Show*, my mother would take each of us
into the only bathroom in our house and scrub us down. She'd
either put us in the tub and give us a thorough once-over, or
she'd wash our hair and faces in the sink—spending inordinate
washcloth time on our necks and behind our ears. By the time she
was done, we were as spic-and-span clean as the kettles and pans
in her kitchen cupboards.

On Sunday morning, we'd get up early and race to see who
could get to the Sunday funnies first. Then we'd take turns slowly
perusing our favorite comics by the heater. This would all come
to an abrupt halt when our mother realized what time it was and
hustled to get us moving so we wouldn't be late. We'd scramble
to get on our Sunday best, which for the boys included a white
shirt, sports coat, and tie. We'd then pack off in our station
wagon and head for church.

In church, we would sit, make a minimal effort to sing along
in the hymnals, and sit some more. The words of the speaker
would drone on, our little bottoms would start to go numb, and

the mental and physical anguish would settle in. We would look for any slight crumb of entertainment to relieve the boredom. We'd play with our dad's watch, look through the papers and fuzz in our pockets, and try to get one another to laugh. Every so often we'd briefly peek up from our seats to hear the source of the endless "blah, blah, blah." We'd quickly check out the clock to see if it had budged, beg to go to the bathroom, canvass the activities of other inmates in the vicinity, fidget, and then sit some more.

Church wasn't fun, but it was simple and clear-cut. And if we didn't pick up a lot, it didn't matter much. Most of our neighbors and friends held similar values. Good (helping others) was right, and bad (harming others) was wrong. Television programs and the movies were made as much for kids as they were for adults. Mighty Mouse, the Lone Ranger, and Popeye were good; Bluto, Boris, and Natasha were diabolical. There hadn't been gangs, widespread drug use, a sexual revolution, or ongoing graphic violence on TV or at the movies (nor was there as much real violence in society itself). The self-discipline, sacrifice, and restraint of the World War II generation naturally gave way to the less disciplined lifestyle of a more prosperous and individualistic postwar generation.

> According to Gallup research, 89 percent of Americans would want a child of theirs to receive religious education, and many Americans believe that the best place for it is in the home.

To a certain degree, what we gained in freedom and material well-being, we lost in restraint and discipline.

Since the 1960s, violence, crime, drug use, and teen sexual activity have increased dramatically. Between 1960 and 1998, violent crime and general crime rates increased by 352 percent and 245 percent respectively. In 1962 four million Americans said they tried an illegal drug; by 1998 the number had grown to seventy-eight million. Between 1960 and 1996, live births to unwed teen mothers increased by 418 percent. In the context of this societal change, moral grounding has become even more important for our children. All of a sudden, it *does* matter if our children don't get the religious and moral training that we used to get from church, since we can't assume that they'll automatically pick up a good sense of right and wrong from our larger society.

While surveys over the past few decades consistently show that approximately 40 percent of the U.S. population attends church, temple, or other religious institutions regularly, this percentage appears to be decreasing for young people. According to research from the Institute of Social Research at the University of Michigan, the percentage of high school seniors who attend church regularly has declined from 41 percent in 1976 to 33 percent by 1996. If this is true, roughly two thirds of high school seniors are getting their religious and moral training outside of church, which is fine if parents are taking direct responsibility for that education. But if parents aren't providing it, our children will pick up many of their religious and moral cues from the media and from peer groups, for better or worse.

One of our most important parental responsibilities, for the benefit of our children and their future world, is to teach them the beliefs and values that will help them to be happy and to do good. For theists, or believers in God (about 96 percent of the U.S. population), key beliefs include those about God. Polls conducted by Gallup International in 1998 indicate that approximately 89 percent of Americans would like a child of theirs to have religious instruction. Past surveys also suggest that a significant number of Americans believe home is the best place for religious training. If we truly believe that religious and moral instruction is important, then we need to figure out how to deliver.

Not feeling comfortable with the doctrines or structures of organized religion isn't a good enough reason not to teach our own children about religion and morality—any more than feeling uncomfortable with public education would be a good reason not to give our children adequate academic and vocational training. There is nothing to stop us from teaching our children ourselves. Feeling that religion and morality are culturally "unhip" is an even worse reason for not teaching our children. We need to put aside cultural and intellectual correctness and focus on the well-being of our children.

We can offer religious and moral training at home whether we've found a comfortable place within organized religion or not. Religious institutions can't replace the influence of our own beliefs, teachings, and example. If we want our children to pick up on the values that are most important to us, we need to take direct responsibility for teaching and living those values. If we want our kids to have gratitude and reverence for God, we need to express that gratitude and reverence in the home. Organized religion can be helpful, but it can't replace the role of the parent as the primary moral guide and mentor.

Every child has the right to be taught about God and moral law.

—BILLY GRAHAM

"Home Churching" as a Cornerstone

The family is, so to speak, the domestic church. In it, parents should, by their word and example, be the first [teachers] of the faith to their children.

—POPE PAUL VI

OVER THE YEARS, MY WIFE AND I HAVE GRADUALLY MOVED IN the direction of making our home the centerpiece of our religious and moral training. Our good, witty friend Lindsey once somewhat jokingly referred to our home-oriented approach to religion as "home churching." The term isn't quite right. We don't have a church in our home and our approach to religious and moral training is mostly informal. But it was a quick and catchy phrase that stuck with us. What the term has come to mean for us is simply providing religious and moral training in the home. Some parents carry out this training by participating in organized religion and reinforcing their faith tradition in the home. Others simply strive to set a good example and have informal conversations with their children from time to time. These can both be powerful approaches to benefiting our children's lives.

In our case, we stumbled toward our own hybrid approach to this training. Even before having children, our relationship with organized religion had shifted. We had changed from viewing this relationship as a subservient, "adult-to-child" relationship with an institution, to seeing it as an "adult-to-adult" relationship with other people of faith. We had shifted from more formal to less formal, from more involvement to less involvement. Despite this shift, with our first child we depended more heavily on church-based training. This was consistent with how we had been raised. But when our incredulous son started asking me questions like "Dad, they said that God sent a plague and killed a bunch of people. Do *you* believe that?" or "Dad, they said that God drowned almost all of the people on the earth. Do *you* believe that?," I realized that I had to think more about these things and get involved. I respected the sincere beliefs of those who were passing along these stories in literal ways, but I had sincere beliefs, too, and they were the ones I most wanted my children to learn. We were the type of squeamish parents who felt compelled to tell our son the truth about Santa Claus when he asked us about the issue point-blank, so that he wouldn't equate ultimate disappointment in Santa with disappointment in God (we thereafter explained Santa's identity as a "fun surprise" to our younger children, so that they could still enjoy the excitement of Christmas morning).

So if we didn't like the idea of God as Santa Claus, God as a benevolent version of Genghis Khan was well off our charts. On the one hand, we had been telling our son that God loved His children and wanted us to be kind to people; on the other hand, he was being taught that every so often God would do very mean things to His children if they didn't do what He asked. The wise and loving God of our belief system was being trans-

> Whether or not we have a strong affiliation with organized religion, the home and family—however we define those terms—need to be the cornerstone of our religious and moral lives.

formed into a mostly nice but sometimes pretty mean god—more medieval monarch than Creator and Provider of the universe. I knew better. I had experienced the love of a great father and mother, and I believed that God had to be at least as wise and good as my own two parents.

Much like parents who aren't entirely comfortable with their children's academic training and choose to get involved with it, we decided we needed to get more directly involved with our children's religious and moral training. Despite the kind efforts of teachers at church, we wanted to increase our influence. Thus began an evolution for our family toward this notion of home churching. This process began by occasionally having informal discussions with our children around the kitchen table and reading stories together. We started having more prayers together as a family. It eventually led us to brief weekly family devotionals, and making those devotionals and other simple family-based traditions the centerpiece of family religious life. We have maintained a connection with organized religion, but with a lighter touch. The Amish have a custom of gathering together with other families on one Sunday, and staying home with their own family the next. We have loosely adopted this custom by participating in the "gathering church" (organized religion) every other week or so. Organized religion, from our perspective, is a support to our personal and family religious experience.

In recent years, I have grown to appreciate the Vatican II comments of Pope Paul VI included at the beginning of this chapter. While the pope undoubtedly had his own faith in mind, the notion of making the domestic church a primary vehicle to teach our own children is compelling for people of all faiths. The positive beliefs and attitudes we pass on to our children in the home can be powerful and positive influences in their lives.

As our family religious life evolved in this direction, I became more interested in family-based religion on an academic level. Over a year's time, I conducted research on the topic at the library of the Graduate Theological Union, near the University of California at Berkeley. What I discovered was quite amazing (I've provided a brief synopsis of some of my findings in the appendix). I found that the first teachers of religion were fathers and mothers. The original religious leaders of the Hebrew tribes, for example, weren't full-time priests and prophets but the patri-archs—the heads of clans. The everyday religions of ancient Rome and China were completely family-based, and the officia-tors of those religious traditions were parents. I learned that fam-ily religion has been the most fundamental and traditional form of religion throughout much of human history. Over time, clans and families adopted organized, institutional religions as their family religions of choice. But for a long while, organized religion remained secondary to the family and its culture when it came to family worship and instruction. Even today, much of the religious activity in India, Asia, and Africa is home- or family-based.

I have come to believe that regardless of whether we have a strong affiliation with organized religion, the home and family—however we define those terms—need to be the cornerstone of our religious and moral lives. In modern theological parlance, our domestic church needs to be at least as fundamental to our spiri-tual lives as the gathering church, if not more so.

Where does love begin? In our own homes.

—MOTHER TERESA

Spirituality and Religion

CHILDREN HAVE INTERESTING WAYS OF DELVING INTO THE
big questions of religion and life. One day my son Jackson went
to a local drugstore with his mother. As they rode home, he
stared out the car window, deep in thought. Finally, he sat up and
announced, "I've got two really big questions." As my wife read-
ied herself to respond, he said, "First of all, where did God come
from? And second of all, where did Payless Drugstore get its
name?" The second was the much easier question to answer.

Our children sometimes force us to think seriously about our
own views on spirituality and religion. As a baby boomer, I've
been amazed in recent years to see how many members of my
generation have started using terms like "spiritual" and "spirituality." I expect we'll continue to place higher value on spiritual
themes as our baby-boomer bodies age and our sweet spirits
become more and more attractive by comparison. For the purposes of this book, I need to define what I mean when I use the
terms "spirituality" and "religion." I refer to our spiritual lives as
simply our interior lives—our awareness, beliefs, thoughts, feelings, intuitions, memories, and imaginations. Spirituality is the
degree to which we're in touch with that interior life, find it
important, and work to strengthen and enrich it. For theists, that

interior life includes our beliefs and feelings about God and the larger Creation. For many theists, it also includes their relationship and experiences *with* God and God's universe.

I define good spiritual health as a state of inner resilience, well-being, and a desire to do good through helping others and refraining from harm. For theists, a full spiritual life includes having trust in God and a sense of the sacred. From my perspective, helping our children spiritually is much more than reading Bible stories to them—it encompasses the whole gamut of helping them to develop beliefs, thinking habits, and behavior that contributes to their inner well-being. It includes loving them, being kind to them, teaching them right from wrong, offering them healthy beliefs about themselves and the world, giving them some occasional firmness, and helping them to develop self-discipline and helpfulness. The proper measure of our children's spiritual health isn't how much they talk about religion, but the general level of happiness and commitment to goodness they display— and, for theists, the level of trust they have in God. We enrich our children's internal (spiritual) lives whenever we influence their beliefs, thinking habits, and behavior in ways that bring them inner well-being and prompt them to do good.

Religion, as I use the word in this book, refers to specific systems of belief that relate to our views of the ultimate source and purpose of our existence. These systems are generally created and driven by a desire to acknowledge and revere God (or the Power behind the Creation), determine how God would want us to live, live in harmony with that determination, and anticipate what might become of us after we die. Religion can be very personal—

> Spirituality is the degree to which we're in touch with our interior life, find it important, and work to strengthen and enrich it. For theists, that interior life includes our beliefs and feelings about God and the larger Creation.

our own individualized belief system—or it can be more collective, as with the belief systems of organized religions. At its best, organized religion contributes to personal faith and to communal worship of God in a supportive, comforting, and inspiring way. At its worst, organized religion becomes an end unto itself, setting itself up in an authoritative brokerage relationship between God and man, and sometimes developing systems and traditions that are unnecessarily harsh and burdensome.

In his seminal work *Varieties of Religious Experience*, American philosopher and psychologist William James found that many experiences of the spirit were common among all religious traditions. Adherents of certain traditions might believe that their inspirations, visions, and faith-promoting experiences were unique, but in fact parallels could be found in most other traditions. This corresponds to Swiss psychologist Carl Jung's view that there is a common spiritual dimension to all people (a "collective unconscious"); that we aren't simply born with a blank slate but that we have a baseline spiritual nature that manifests itself among people around the world in different ways. It also corresponds to recollections of people who have had near-death events—people of all faiths (or no faiths) tend to have very similar experiences. They normally don't return from those experiences with a desire to change religious affiliations, but they almost always come back with a deepened commitment to their personal religious faith. (See, for example, Dr. Michael Sabom's book, *Light and Death*, published by Zondervan in 1998.)

It's important not to equate the life of the spirit solely with religion. The life of the spirit is our interior life, and religion is a belief system that might be *part* of it. Depending on their content, religious beliefs can either add to or detract from our internal well-being. Organized religion is a temporary vehicle, and how well it works for us depends on what it does to support our faith and help us to be happy and do good. As Gandhi taught, "God does not belong to any one religion." We can enrich our children's lives for the long term as we teach them beneficial religious beliefs. If we choose to associate with organized religion, we can also help our children settle into a healthy, mature relationship with a religious organization or tradition that promotes faith, happiness, and goodness.

We are not human beings having a spiritual experience.

We are spiritual beings having a human experience.

—PIERRE TEILHARD DE CHARDIN
(Twentieth-century Jesuit philosopher and scientist)

Morality

The sense of right and wrong is the beginning of wisdom.

—MENCIUS
(Third century B.C. Confucian philosopher)

ONE DAY I WENT OUT TO DO SOME SALMON FISHING WITH MY brothers and brother-in-law in the Pacific Ocean, just off the San Francisco Bay. It turned out to be a very long day with hardly any bites. But then, as we were starting to head back, we finally pulled in a salmon. It looked a little bit scrawny, so we measured it. It was an inch or so shorter than the legal requirement. We hesitated a bit, but not long. We had earned this fish and we weren't about to put it back. As we rolled under the Golden Gate Bridge and headed into Sausalito, we saw, to our astonishment, a Fish and Game boat inspecting fishing boats (something that had never happened to us in all of our many "legal" trips). Just as we might have done when we were little boys, we tried to nonchalantly glide over to the dock and act like nothing had happened. One of my brothers hopped out of the boat to get his truck. We started to clean up the boat and pretended not to notice the Fish and Game inspector as he sauntered up by us. "Catch anything?" he queried. "Not really," we fudged with surprising lack of hesitation. As he and we spotted the fish scales in the bottom of the boat at the same time, he said, "Okay, what's up?" I blurted out, "Oh yeah, there was the one fish." We pulled out our scrawny fish and he measured it. In Three Stooges fashion, we began explaining our situation with bumbling stories, and when my brother returned with his truck, he gave a brand-new version of our woeful tale. The inspector got so disgusted that he fined us all. All three of us, grown adults who normally hold high ideals like honesty, ended up admitting to our delinquent behavior before a county judge. I've reminded my children of the moral of this story, so they know that telling "fish" stories is not a good idea and there can be real consequences for not telling the truth.

Despite the emotional charge that surrounds the word "morality," it's actually a simple concept. To paraphrase William James, science says that things are; morality says that some things are better than others; and religion says that the truly better things are eternal and can bring happiness even in the here and now. Regardless of what modernists tell us, baseline morality is not relative and subjective. To the contrary, basic human morality is universal—some things are clearly and absolutely better than others in our human world. There are ethical principles that apply across time and cultures. Love is better than hate, honesty is better than dishonesty, and marital fidelity is better than infidelity. We don't need angels to come and tell us what hurts or helps others. God has written a basic moral code into the soul of humanity.

> Morality says that some things are better than others. We don't need angels to come and tell us what hurts or helps others. God has written a basic moral code into the soul of humanity.

For sure, moral codes can get out of hand: they can be unreasonable and too long, and not all moral codes are equal. Some result in great unhappiness and harm in the world. Societal or tribal moral rules maintaining that people are bad if they are of a different race, religion, or economic status have resulted in terrible, hateful behavior throughout human history. Cultural or commercial moral rules maintaining that we're better if we're rich, good-looking, popular, or free of disability undermine our contentment and distort our views of what it means to be human. Strong peer-pressure moral codes that enforce that it's bad to have opinions, wear certain clothing, or have other interests divergent from the peer group's culture can create an environment that fosters ridicule and cruelty. Family moral rules that maintain children are bad if they make trivial mistakes, don't always behave like adults, or have personality traits or opinions different from those of their parents can limit the lifelong happiness and fulfillment of individuals. And soft moral rules maintaining that violence, dishonesty, and sexual promiscuity are acceptable can lead to great disaster for individuals and societies alike.

It's critical to provide rules of right and wrong for our children. But those rules need to be as short and beneficial as possible. As we reinforce clear rules of right and wrong, we must use wisdom and return to the simple moral code written in the soul of humanity and in many of our sacred writings. For example, the simplicity of the Ten Commandments has remained, through the ages, an inspired "shortlist" of serious moral expectations (rules of nonviolence, nonstealing, and sexual restraint). An even more condensed version is the Golden Rule espoused by Jesus and others: treat others as we would want to be treated. The test of natural moral law is "What would the world be like if everyone lived by this rule?" Living true to natural moral law provides for the common good of all people. By teaching our children a core moral code, both by word and deed, we benefit both them and our larger society.

We teach our children most convincingly about morality through our own choices and conduct. In my family, we occasionally talk to our children informally about moral issues that come up in the news and in our life experience, and sometimes we'll talk to them more formally during the family devotionals that we have. But beyond trying to watch our own behavior (fish stories and the like), probably the most important thing we do is to maintain and follow up on simple family rules that prohibit harmful behavior and reinforce our sense of right and wrong.

Learn to do good.

—ISAIAH 1:17

Discipline and Happiness

He who is slow to anger is better than the mighty, and he who
rules his spirit than he who takes a city.

—PROVERBS 16:32

LIVING BY A MORAL CODE REQUIRES DISCIPLINE. TEACHING
our children to refrain from harm not only benefits them and
others in obvious physical and social ways (by keeping them away
from violence, cruelty, drugs, and other negative behavior), but
the discipline involved can also give them greater inner peace.

Discipline is no more (or less) than directing our behavior
toward an aspiration. Until we get the hang of directing that
behavior, discipline is sometimes just plain hard work. When my
son began to do yard work for our family a few years ago, he
hated and fought it. He would sometimes go out of his way to
grouse and cut corners—all natural responses that I recall using
when I was his age. But now his work is easy and efficient. He is
totally unaware of the discipline he has developed. He has even
told me on a few occasions, in moments of weakness, that sometimes he actually enjoys getting out and working in the yard. This
is the wonderful effect that discipline can have in our lives. Without it, we can't achieve our aspirations, and living happily in a tur-
bulent world is much more difficult.

Just instilling in our children the discipline to complete difficult and valued tasks can be a long-term blessing in their lives. In
our family, we give our children chores and other tasks with the
specific purpose of helping them develop a little discipline. My

wife and I ask our children to practice piano, walk the dog, do dishes, clean their rooms consistently, run neighborhood errands, and take on larger summertime responsibilities—not just to help out or become more proficient (though this is part of the goal), but to help them develop discipline. We don't go overboard with these tasks; kids also need time to play, relax, do homework, and just be kids. But we feel asking our children to help with simple family tasks isn't too much to ask, considering the great deal of home-based work that rural children of the past were required to perform.

This type of task-based discipline can help children become more self-reliant and resilient. But when we also help our children develop the discipline to refrain from harm, we benefit society as a whole. Good character is having a fundamental commitment to refrain from harm and to help others. As parents, we need to remember that the bedrock of good character is self-discipline. Without a measure of self-discipline, our children's chances of developing good character are diminished.

> We do our children no favors by simply leading them from one fun event (or one fun toy) to another and shielding them from every discomfort. They will end up being unprepared for life and its trials.

As our children become more acclimated to forgoing their own impulses and comfort to achieve a worthwhile aspiration, they become less attached (or addicted, in extreme cases) to the endless cycle of chasing after the next pleasure and avoiding the next pain. We do our children no favors by simply leading them from one fun event (or one fun toy) to another and shielding them from every discomfort. They will end up being unprepared for life and its trials.

My wife, Julie, has provided one of the most powerful examples I've known for accepting discomfort to achieve one's aspirations. Since the age of twelve, she has had rheumatoid arthritis.

Only those who bear the burden of RA can understand the trial of twenty-four-hour-a-day pain. The basic everyday efforts that most of us take for granted—walking, sitting, and sleeping—can at times be challenging and painful for her. But while Julie does what she can medically to relieve her pain, she doesn't avoid it; she accepts it as part of her much larger life. She leads a very full and active physical life, refusing to avoid the discomfort that would keep her from her aspirations. I try to remember her when I want to avoid doing important things because of a little hunger, a little tiredness, a little pain, or a little irritation.

It's important to remember that discipline doesn't ensure happiness. We've all known people who are absolute "saints" when it comes to living constructive lives and yet don't seem particularly happy. We must also adopt healthy beliefs about ourselves and the world if we are to be happy. If, in our desire to teach our children some discipline, we tell them that they are worthwhile only when they're carrying out tasks and doing good, we can set them up for insecurity and unhappiness. It's critical that our children receive unconditional love and come to accept their humanity and inherent worth. To be happy in their lives requires reasonable, healthy beliefs and thinking habits as well as disciplined, healthy behavior.

Finally, helping our children to develop discipline doesn't mean that they shouldn't have lots of fun and enjoy life. Sometimes I realize, when I look down sternly at my children about an undone chore, that they're fully convinced they're looking back up at "Antifun" incarnated. Or as my daughter, Brooke, put it a few years back (in a very adult way): "It seems like all I do is go to bed, get up, go to school, go to bed, get up, go to school; what's up with that? When do I get to play?" Life without fun and play is unbearable. We should help our children develop the ability not to become so attached to obtaining pleasure and avoiding pain that they don't do things to benefit themselves and others. We all stand a greater chance of sustaining inner well-being if we have mastery over our impulses, our desires, and our actions. But we also can't live without fun.

No man is free who is not master of himself.

—EPICTETUS
(First-century Roman slave and Stoic philosopher)

Figuring Out Our Own Beliefs

Seek, and you will find.
—JESUS (Luke 11:9)

BEFORE WE CAN BEGIN TO TEACH OUR CHILDREN OUR RELIGIOUS
and moral beliefs, we need to make sure we know what they are.
As a person with a natural interest in religious and philosophical
issues, I've spent a lot of time sorting out my beliefs.

I grew up as a Mormon in the small Northern California
wine-industry town of St. Helena, right in the heart of Napa Val-
ley (reared in a family of teetotalers, I was like a kid who doesn't
like to ride on theme-park attractions growing up in Disney
World). Originally, we attended church eighteen miles away in
the larger town of Napa, but eventually we had our own little
group in St. Helena that met in the American Legion Hall. Perhaps because there were so few of us, and since I didn't have any
Mormon friends at first, it was easy for me to feel completely
connected to others of my age in the community. It was a wonderful statement about our town, and about my parents, that I
grew up without any religious or racial sensibility—people were
just people. It wasn't until I was ten or eleven that it dawned on
me there were even different religions. I had always assumed my
friends went to different buildings for church but that we all
believed the same things and we were all still part of the same
basic church (of course, I also believed that the famed "golden
plates" of Mormonism were to be found in one of the American
Legion Hall's closets).

Maybe because of my early plural-
istic experience and my innate interest in seriously examining the big
questions of life, from adolescence
on—including time spent serving a
Spanish-speaking Mormon mission
in inner-city Chicago—I struggled
with specific religious doctrines. I
seemed to have been born with a
basic belief in God, and as a person

> Figuring out what we
> believe is the critical
> first step to training
> our children. Before
> we can teach them
> our beliefs, we need
> to confirm what they
> are.

who enjoyed athletics and family, I greatly appreciated the Mormon emphasis on healthy living and family solidarity. My religious upbringing reinforced my faith in God and gave me a good
moral anchor. But as with other historic faiths that I subsequently
studied, certain beliefs and practices didn't seem reasonable or
right to me on either an emotional or a logical level. For many
people, the religious institution of their birth is a naturally comfortable and complete fit, and they do not have this struggle. I
have come to appreciate the wisdom of the Dalai Lama, who
wrote in *The Art of Happiness*:

In this world, there are so many different people, so many
dispositions. There are five billion human beings [now six bil-
lion] and in a certain way I think we need five billion different
religions, because there is such a variety of dispositions. I
believe that each individual should embark upon a spiritual
path that is best suited to his or her mental disposition, natural inclination, temperament, belief, family, and cultural
background. Now, for example, as a Buddhist monk, I find
Buddhism most suitable. But that does not mean that Buddhism is best for everyone. That's clear. It's definite. If I
believed that Buddhism were best for everyone, that would be
foolish, because different people have different mental dispositions. So the variety of people calls for a variety of religions.

The purpose of religion is to benefit people, and I think that if we only had one religion, after a while it would cease to benefit many people. . . .

The very positive aspect of my personal struggle was to ultimately reconfirm my own direct, independent faith in God as the foundation of my religious belief. It ensured that God, and not institutions, would be the focus of my belief and worship. I've been able to figure out exactly what I believe and why. This in turn has helped me to achieve the solid grounding that I need to teach my own children. I've also developed a more comfortable perspective on the role that organized religion can play in our lives and the positive influence it can have if it so chooses. A structured religious experience can help formalize and reinforce our children's worship of God and their personal moral commitments. It can provide them with a supportive and helpful community of faith. I remain respectful of the religion of my "clan" because it has been the revered religion of my family group for several generations now and has helped to reinforce general faith and morality. I also remain respectful of the religious faith of my more remote ancestors (pre-Christians, Catholics, Lutherans, Anglicans, and Quakers alike). But the specifics of my personal faith remain independent from my traditional family religion or any other organized religion. My core faith is simply in God.

Figuring out what we believe is the critical first step to training our children. Before we can teach them our beliefs, we need to confirm what they are. There are three basic avenues to obtaining and confirming belief and knowledge: (1) reason (including common sense); (2) experience; and (3) insight (aka inspiration, intuition). For some people, evidence that appeals to reason is more important; for others, direct experience or insight speaks more strongly. For William James, evidence of God came not from the exterior world but "lies primarily in inner personal experiences." For Albert Einstein, the wonder of the mathematical formula

FIGURING OUT OUR OWN BELIEFS

behind our universe, and the implied "superior reasoning power," provided evidence for his idea of God (the "illimitable superior spirit"). For me, all three avenues of confirming belief have been of value. I have studied and reasoned enough to be convinced that intelligent design is behind the universe, that mind is special, and that people have an innate spiritual nature. On occasion I have had profound inner personal experiences, including the peace that sometimes comes from prayer and meditation as well as moments of connectedness to God and the Creation and greater awareness of the sacred in our everyday world. I have also had a few tangible outer experiences of the spirit that convince me there is more to this world than meets the eye (including having our two-year-old son confirm that our second son was on his way and what his name was going to be—even before we knew that Julie was once again pregnant and even though we had never told our son the name we had indeed thought to give another son). I have come to know people who have experienced near-death events and I've been persuaded of the reality of what they experienced (including a friend whose heart stopped for several minutes and he entered a realm of light and tangible peace, resulting in the removal of his lifelong fear of death). And every so often I have received flashes of insight that support some of my beliefs on an intuitive basis. My faith is by no means perfect, any more than my knowledge of many things is perfect. But I have come to agree with Jesus that if we seek, we will find—that although we may not find everything, we will find enough to see us through. I have also come to believe that the more we can use these three avenues directly—without unquestioning reliance on other "authorities" and intermediaries—the stronger our convictions will be. Because of the special emotional hold that early religious beliefs can have on us, it's important to be mindful of, and account for, those feelings as we explore our beliefs.

Why not take at least a brief period in your life to consciously examine or reconfirm your religious and moral beliefs and values?

There are a number of activities that you can undertake to do this:

- You can take pen to paper and write out what you currently believe (both in terms of religion and your moral code) and why you have those beliefs.
- You can also list areas of uncertainty that you'd like to explore further.
- You can compare your current beliefs with what you've observed in life, what you've experienced, what you've read, and what generally makes sense to you.
- You can read further. I've listed some current books that support theism at the end of this chapter. The sacred writings of the major religions (listed in the appendix) are available to us through our public libraries. I also recommend Huston Smith's book *The World's Religions*, published in 1991 by HarperSanFrancisco, for a general overview of the world's major religions.
- You can talk to trusted family members, friends, and full-time religious people (ministers, priests, rabbis, and religious educators).
- You can visit churches, temples, mosques, and other institutions and participate in their services.
- You can pray and meditate and observe your own insights and inner experiences with respect to these matters.

To help yourself in this process, you can also ask yourself any number of simple questions:

- Do you believe in a supreme being, a universal spirit, or a greater spiritual or natural power behind the universe?
- What kind of God makes sense to you?
- If you were raised within a particular organized religion, do you still consider it your primary source of spiritual enrichment? Is it "who you are"?

- ■■ Have you learned enough about other religions to decide whether to weave other elements into your personal religion?
- ■■ What basic rules of right and wrong do you want your children to live by?

Your kids, of course, will be more direct. What will you say when they ask:

- ■■ Do you believe in God?
- ■■ What happens after we die?
- ■■ Is there such a thing as heaven? How do you get there? Will our dog go there?
- ■■ Is there such a thing as hell? How do you get there?
- ■■ Do our loved ones who have died watch over us?

Belief isn't knowledge, so it's only natural for any subject to have shades and degrees of belief and doubt. And as Immanuel Kant, a theistic German philosopher, argued so convincingly over two hundred years ago, even human knowledge can never be absolute. For sure, there are facts and experience that we can depend on in this life. We can be absolutely convinced of many things. But we simply don't know what kind of knowledge and experience lie beyond our human experience; we're constrained by our human understanding and condition.

Sometimes people are so focused on not making errors in their search for truth that they reject any belief that isn't certain. By being so intellectually stingy, such people can also lose out on important truths that might have brought them greater happiness. They are, as William James pointed out, not unlike the bachelor who chooses not to propose to the woman he loves in order to make sure he doesn't make a mistake. While he might ensure his infallibility, he also risks missing out on some of the most wonderful possibilities of his life (see James's helpful little book *The Will to Believe*). A belief that isn't 100 percent certain may still be extremely valuable if it's believable *enough* and brings happiness and goodness to our lives. Maybe it's worth the risk to try new rules: instead of not believing ideas of a religious nature until they're proven 100 percent true (which isn't realistic anyway), why not take a chance on some reasonable religious and moral beliefs until they're proven false?

Many millions search for God and find Him in their hearts.

— SIKH PROVERB

Recent Books in Support of a Theistic Worldview

Borg, Marcus. *Meeting Jesus Again for the First Time*. San Francisco: HarperSanFrancisco, 1994. (For Christian-oriented parents who struggle with "literalness" issues in Christianity.)

Dembski, William A. and Michael J. Behe. Downers Grove, IL: *Intelligent Design*. Intervarsity Press, 1999.

Denton, Michael J. *Nature's Destiny*. New York: The Free Press, 1998.

Glynn, Patrick. *God the Evidence*. Rocklin, IL: Prima Publishing, 1999.

Herbert, N. *Quantum Reality*. Garden City, NY: Anchor Press, 1988.

Polkinghorne, John. *Belief in God in an Age of Science*. New Haven, CT: Yale University Press, 1998.

Reagan, Michael, ed. *The Hand of God*. Kansas City, MO: Andrews McMeel, 1999.

Schafer, Lothar. *In Search of Divine Reality*. Fayetteville, AR: University of Arkansas Press, 1997.

Spetner, Lee M. *Not By Chance*. Brooklyn, NY: The Judaica Press, 1998.

Swinborne, Richard. *Is There a God?* Oxford: Oxford University Press, 1997.

Templeton, John Marks, ed. *Evidence of Purpose*. New York: Continuum Publishing, 1994.

———. *How Large Is God?* Philadelphia: Templeton Foundation Press, 1997.

The Limits of Science

Science can purify religion from error and superstition; religion can
purify science from idolatry and false absolutes.

—JOHN PAUL II

ONE EVENING I CAME HOME LATE FROM WORK TO FIND MY SON
Adam dutifully working on some science homework at the
kitchen table. As I passed by on my way to the refrigerator, I
noticed that he was working with the same type of human evolution timeline that I had studied in school. Since Julie had mostly
handled the "where do babies come from" discussions in our
home, I thought it was only natural that the "where did *people*
come from" discussion should fall to my manly shoulders—and
this was clearly the momentous occasion for my wisdom. I had
kept somewhat abreast of evolutionary theory, and so I sat down
and explained to Adam some of the strengths and weaknesses of
modern thought about evolution (including weaknesses in the
simple "homo erectus to neanderthal to homo sapiens" chart in
front of us). I expounded on the explanatory limitations of natural
selection and random mutation in ways that I was sure would
impress. I expressed my "bottom line" core belief that for me,
regardless of the natural processes involved in the creation of the
world and people (processes that can never be fully understood), a
supernatural source, God, was behind it all. Adam's polite
response was, in essence, "That's swell, Dad, but I'm actually just
trying to finish my homework."

As we, and our children, strive to figure out our own beliefs, it's only natural that we will cross paths with the world of science, and that some of us will want to consider ideas coming out of science in support of our beliefs. But it's also important to understand the limits of science in this process. These limits come from two important facts. First of all, we are indeed constrained, as Kant pointed out, by our human understanding and condition. We never know what kind of knowledge or existence is beyond our human grasp. And second, "real" science itself is limited in its scope. As Sir Karl Popper, the eminent philosopher of science, pointed out, a truly scientific theory is one that can be tested—if you can't figure out a physical test that can be used to disprove a theory, it's not "scientific." Many theories about the past and future are not strictly "scientific" (including major ones like Big Bang and Macro-evolution), since there is no way to conclusively test and disprove them. Science is confined to the repeatable and testable. It's wonderful that scientists pursue their most educated guesses as to how natural processes have influenced the universe, and there is value in doing so, but we need to remember that these are still guesses, always subject to change. These limitations should humble scientist and cleric alike. We all ultimately walk by faith, no matter who we are.

> It's one thing to believe that an electron or two could be produced by blind chance, but all the laws, substances, and complex designs we find in the universe?

Because of these limits, there is no way to scientifically "prove" our religious beliefs, though it sometimes seems like we can come very close. Personally, I believe that there is a superfluous amount of evidence in the universe for God. The odds of this enormous, complicated, synchronized, mathematically based universe coming into existence as the result of chance is, as astronomer Hugh Ross points out, about as likely as "a Boeing 747 aircraft being completely assembled as the result of a tornado striking a junkyard." It's one thing to believe that an electron or two could be produced by blind chance, but all the laws, substances, and complex designs we find in the universe? Or as Alan Sandage, winner of the Crawford Prize in astronomy and a nontheist turned theist (at age fifty), has put it: "It was my science that drove me to the conclusion that the world is more complicated than can be explained by science. It is only through the supernatural that I can understand the mystery of existence." But I realize that the details of our universe represent only evidence for a Creator, and not "scientific proof," since there is no available physical test that can disprove God's existence.

While schools and universities don't necessarily need to teach our specific beliefs about God, we need to ensure that our schools are respectful of our most cherished beliefs. Depending on our beliefs, it may be important to go in and talk to our children's teachers. If, for example, we hold strong fundamental beliefs about the Bible that run counter to scientific points of view that are being taught in our school, we should go in and figure out with our teacher how to ensure that our beliefs are respected and that our children are taught in a way that we're comfortable with. This is too difficult an issue for our children to work out on their own with their teachers.

Though it hasn't come up often, whenever my children bring home ideas from school that provide explanations of life and the universe that leave God out of the picture, I remind them not only of the limits of science (and of how "absolutely certain" each generation's scientific theories and books always are, only to be replaced by the next generation's "really, really, absolutely, certain" theories and books), but I also restate my abiding belief in the creative power of Intelligent Design (God) over the creative power of nothingness and chance. If I'm in a hurry and don't have the time to explain my beliefs in more detail, I sometimes say such things as "scientists make educated guesses about the past, but nobody really knows for sure how things got here; for me it doesn't really matter because for me God is behind it all"; or "the laws, design, and details of the universe and life are way too complicated and amazing to explain by chance—for me, intelligent design is a much better explanation than saying that this all happened by accident," or, "sometimes scientists act as though they know things that they don't really know, and it's always important not to just take their words for things; we're all limited by our human understanding and we all walk by faith—even scientists," or "the truth of the matter is that most theories about the past and future aren't scientific since there's no way to conclusively test or disprove them—it's fine to make educated guesses, but they're still guesses."

I have a young friend who went through a few years of darkness and despair. Things were actually going quite well in his life, but he started reading a little philosophy and science and had tentatively concluded that life was pointless and hopeless (a little too much Nietzsche can do that for most anybody). As one who has enjoyed reading about philosophy and science, I'm always saddened when people take the writings of particularly pessimistic philosophers and scientists too seriously, especially when it comes to the ultimate questions of life. Fortunately, my young friend read and thought further and eventually returned to "life." But he went through a very unhappy period purely because of the ideas of prominent, pessimistic people with a Ph.D. next to their names. Understanding the role and limits of science and scientists can be important for our children's inner well-being.

Sometimes our culture has overemphasized our physical and material world at the expense of our spiritual lives. Our most important beliefs aren't scientific or materialistic at all. Our interior (spiritual) world is made better by beliefs that help us to be happy and to do good. I believe the world currently has greater need of spiritual and moral progress than scientific progress. We have focused so much on material well-being that we have sometimes lost sight of what is good for the soul. Our beliefs about God, morality, and continued life after death may not technically qualify as scientific hypotheses, but they nonetheless can be supported by strong personal evidence that leaves us with little doubt. The evidence that comes from reason, real-life experience, and insight (inspiration, intuition) is what "proves" our spiritual beliefs for us. This evidence may not be scientifically conclusive, but it can be powerfully convincing:

- We can see design and order in the universe for ourselves.
- We can look out and reason for ourselves that the enormity, complexity, synchronization, and design of the universe and life can't simply come from nothingness or chance (even more fundamentally, as Alan Sandage kept asking himself, "Why is there something instead of nothing?").
- We can study the numerical basis upon which the universe is devised and understand that the basis of the material world is ultimately nonmaterial (according to quantum physics, the entire universe is resting on a foundation of quantum waves that carry no energy or mass—they are waves only of possibility with content made up of numerical, "mindlike" relationships).
- We can directly experience the amazing details and wonder of this physical world, and our internal spiritual nature (including mind), for ourselves.
- We can experience the power of love, wisdom, beauty, and courage for ourselves.
- We can receive comfort, strength, inspiration, and peace through prayer and meditation for ourselves.
- Some of us have very tangible personal experiences of the spirit for ourselves that can't be defined or constrained by the physical world.

And we can ultimately decide for ourselves which religious beliefs leave us with greater potential for happiness, hope, and doing good in the world: Nontheism or Theism, Materialism or Spirituality.

A commonsense interpretation of the facts suggests that a superintellect has monkeyed with physics, as well as chemistry and biology, and that there are no blind forces worth speaking about in nature. The numbers one calculates from the facts seem to me so overwhelming as to put the conclusion almost beyond question.

—SIR FRED HOYLE
(British astronomer and mathematician)

Teaching Our Unique Beliefs

Remember that you are unique. Your beauty is special; no one on the earth looks exactly like you. God knows you for what you are.

—RUMI
(Thirteenth-century Sufi philosopher and poet)

AS WE RECONFIRM AND DEVELOP OUR BELIEFS OVER TIME (whether religious, cultural, or otherwise), we may find that we have developed heartfelt personal beliefs that are both unique and very important to us—beliefs that nobody will ever pass along to our children if we don't. One of the advantages of a commitment to home churching is that it helps us take a more conscious responsibility for ensuring that our children are taught these beliefs.

For example, I have a belief that most organized religions (and probably the majority of believers) don't share. While I believe that God is ultimately the Creator of our physical world, I also believe that He has purposely limited His role in our mortal world and rarely "physically" intervenes in it. I don't believe, say, that God miraculously plucks one person safely from an airline crash and leaves the others to die, or that God listened to the prayers of a few at Auschwitz and allowed them to survive while ignoring the desperate pleas of so many men, women, and children brutally put to death there. I believe that God would save us all from pain and suffering if that were our purpose for being here—but it clearly is not. At least part of our purpose in being here is to experience a fully natural world, with a measure of

> We may find that
> we have developed
> heartfelt personal
> beliefs that are both
> unique and very
> important to us—
> beliefs that nobody
> will ever pass along
> to our children if
> we don't.

physical and moral freedom, without God's controlling intervention. We all feel from time to time that life isn't fair. But maybe the only way that life can be fair, while still allowing for a measure of physical and moral freedom, is for it to be a somewhat *random*, natural existence that we must all participate in without any guarantees. For me, God's mercy doesn't come in the form of physical intervention when things don't go well, but rather in making sure that our stay in this natural world—and its associated suffering and difficulty—doesn't last any longer than it should. It's as though God has said, "Okay, for your long-term benefit I'll let you have a taste of a natural, mortal world, a taste of joy, a taste of human freedom, but there's no way you can fully understand the pain that will also be involved. I can't bear and you can't bear to have this go on for too long." I believe that God understands our suffering in this world. I believe that God can provide us with peace and comfort in such a world, that He offers spiritual influence, and that as spiritual beings we have access to spiritual gifts (and that sometimes these gifts and influences may take on very real and tangible form). But as a general rule, my faith in God isn't believing that God will give us what we want if we just believe hard enough; it's trusting in God through the "thick and thin" of life.

Because this belief is important to me, I share it informally with my children when tragedies happen and the survival of a few is ascribed to God. On those occasions, I'll say something like "God has made a natural world, and part of being in a natural world is to have both good and bad things happen." Or "God doesn't cause bad things to happen, they're just part of a natural world." Or "Remember, God loves us and understands our suffering; and as hard as this life can sometimes be for people, it doesn't last forever." A belief that God regularly intervenes in miraculous ways in our physical world makes sense to many people, and I respect that (indeed, if this is how life is, all the better). But I also need to be true to my own beliefs and share them with my children, no matter how far out of the religious mainstream I may be.

Sometimes children bring home ideas that run counter to our unique beliefs. They might say, "That's not what we learned in school" or "That's not what we learned in Sunday school." My approach to this situation is to respectfully tell my children what I believe and why, and then ask them what they think (I think asking our kids their opinions is important not only in terms of reinforcing their value, but also in understanding where they are with things). I also try to reinforce with my children that sincere people will have differing opinions about all sorts of things in life.

Through various means, I've tried to encourage our children to think on their own when it comes to things they learn at school, church, or any other place. I've told them I don't expect them to believe as I do on everything, but they also shouldn't automatically accept what they hear from "experts" at school or in the media. I still love Richard Feynman's great simple question: "How did they find that out?" Asking your child that question is a wonderful way to help him or her think critically about the information and opinions that we're given in life.

Undoubtedly, you have beliefs and opinions that are important and unique to you—not just in the realm of religion and morality, but also in the realms of academics, work, and other aspects of living. Some may be fairly independent beliefs that nobody will pass on to your children unless you do. If you simply send your children off to church or school, they may learn things that are in direct conflict with the beliefs that you hold most dear. We need to ensure that we directly participate in providing our children with the religious and moral training that we believe in—especially those beliefs that are most important and unique to us.

As our case is new, so we must think anew and act anew.

—ABRAHAM LINCOLN

When Parents Have Differing Beliefs

A man shall leave his father and mother and be joined to his wife
and the two shall become one.

—JESUS (Matthew 19:5)

IT'S NOT REASONABLE TO EXPECT THAT WHEN TWO PEOPLE
come together in marriage, they will have the same beliefs about
life, about people, about child-rearing, or about the details of religion. To lesser or greater degrees, all of our marriages are interfaith and intercultural. Even if we come from the same faith
tradition, our exact image of God, intensity of belief, and view of
specific doctrines and practices can be quite different. My wife
and I have very similar beliefs. We both tend to be people of simple, independent faith, and our differences in belief are minor. It's
relatively easy for us to achieve religious harmony within our
home. Probably our biggest area of compromise has been over
how much we participate in organized religion (my personality is
such that I prefer less). But we have known couples who have
been able to attain religious harmony even when their differences
in belief are greater. One husband who was raised as a strict
Catholic has chosen to participate in his wife's Protestant tradition along with their children, though without forsaking his
Catholic roots. His wife has graciously limited their formal participation and is respectful and complimentary of her husband's
faith tradition both with others and with their children. It's clear
from observing their interaction that their love and respect for

each other comes first, and their faith traditions second. The religious harmony in their home comes from empathizing, compromising, and maintaining a firm commitment to each other. It also comes from a mutual desire to provide an approach that works well for their children.

Our core beliefs about religion and morality can be very powerful—they can shape our rules for living and affect our behavior and happiness. If, as parents, we have strong differences of opinion on these matters, we must sit down together and figure out how we will teach our children, rather than simply calling a "truce" and not teaching them anything at all. We need to determine the key beliefs that we can teach in unity.

Most couples agree on core moral beliefs. While there may be many individualistic paths of religious belief, serious, baseline rights and wrongs are clear-cut. Religious beliefs are trickier, requiring even more conscious communication, planning, and decision-making. Experts in the field of interfaith family life emphasize that if couples have very strong disagreements on religion, they need to sit down, explore the details of those disagreements, and come up with a solution for providing religious training. It's much healthier to accept those differences and find common ground, or at least a workable solution, than it is to deny or fight over them.

> If, as parents, we have strong differences of opinion on these matters, we must sit down together and figure out how we will teach our children, rather than simply calling a "truce" and not teaching them anything at all.

I believe in three fundamental rules when it comes to sharing differences in religious belief with our children (or differences in any belief, for that matter): (1) honor and support each other as parents; (2) determine and emphasize the core beliefs we hold in common and can teach in unity; and (3) consciously avoid belittling a spouse's point of view. My personal bias is that we need to help our children develop a primary religious identity as God's children, and secondarily (if applicable) as a Catholic, Protestant, Jew, Moslem, or other formal religious identification. This primary identity binds us to people of different faiths, including members of our own family.

Here are some additional thoughts, based in part on the ideas of interfaith specialists:

■ ■ Whether we participate in organized religion, belong to different faiths, or associate with no faith tradition at all, home should be the foundation of our children's religious and moral training and parents should be the mentors of the tradition, no matter how sporadic or informal that training is. However we deal with the traditions of our respective clans, we first need to figure out a way to provide some religious and moral training within our own families.

■ ■ If one parent has strong religious beliefs and the other does not, consider adopting as your single "family" religion the organized religion of the parent with the stronger religious beliefs. You don't have to agree with everything in an organized religion to associate with it. In our everyday lives, we readily associate with companies, schools, political parties, labor unions, communities, and countries, even though we don't always agree with all the details of what goes on with those groups. We do so because, on balance, they're of value to us and our families.

■ ■ If one of you is a theist and the other is a nontheist or agnostic, make sure you take special pains to determine what you can teach in unity, even if it's only core moral beliefs and values. Find common ground on teaching your children a beneficial moral code. Then come to an agreement on how the theistic parent can pass along his or her religious beliefs to your children in a way that is respectful and supportive of the other spouse. It's still important for a theist to share heartfelt beliefs, while being respectful of his or her spouse, because these beliefs might be very important for children as they sort out their own religious beliefs over time.

A friend of mine was raised as a Catholic and believes in an afterlife. Her husband was raised as a Jew and doesn't believe in an afterlife. She faced the real challenge of their differences in belief when her father-in-law died. Sensing that her heartfelt beliefs might be of comfort to her children during a time of mourning, she shared them while being respectful of her husband's point of view. She went on to explain that "I believe one thing, Dad believes another; we all have our own beliefs; you have to figure out what you believe and have faith in it."

■ ■ If you both have strong but differing religious views, once again, determine what you can teach in unity. Then you can explain the beliefs of your formal faith traditions to your children—the traditions of your clans. Help them understand that the fundamental purpose of all religions is to help us remember God and inspire us to choose to do good. The beauty of different religions is that they do this in ways that relate to the historical, cultural, family, and personality differences of many different people through time. Teach your children the differences of your formal faith traditions, with respect, support, and loyalty for each other. Your children will ultimately learn more about religion and its influence on people's lives by how you treat each other than by what you say about religion. Surveys of interfaith children support the notion that the most important thing to them is having harmony in the home. If you can't settle on a single family religion, then harmoniously attend the services of both religions and participate in the traditions of each with an open heart. Many of us have been enriched by the cultures and traditions of both sides of our families, whether religious or otherwise.

■ ■ If religion is seriously getting in the way of your love and unity, consider religious elopement. Think about finding a different faith tradition that can be all your own. Julie's paternal grandparents were raised on opposite sides of the border between the U.S. and Canada. Sadie Vasseur was part of a strong French-Canadian Catholic clan, and Clayton Britton came from a Scottish-British Protestant family in Maine. Sadie and Clayton began a cross-border courtship, but Sadie's family would not allow their daughter to marry a Protestant. So, to make a wonderful, long story short, Sadie and Clayton eloped. Once all was forgiven, Clayton became his mother-in-law's favorite son-in-law. Sadie and Clayton didn't allow organized religion to get in the way of their love and happiness. Eventually they found their way to a third faith that they could enjoy together. They were more devoted to each other than to the religions of their clans. If religion keeps us from love and devotion to each other, it's not serving its purpose. If your faith keeps you apart, find an approach to religion that brings you together, not one that tears you apart. As the Christian apostle Paul wrote in Romans 8:38, 39, no principalities—including churches—can separate us from the love of God—and they shouldn't separate us from the love of each other.

The work of many people in the field tells us that the keys to good interfaith education in the home are *harmony* and *clarity*. The precise content of the education is less important than parental harmony and commitment to baseline beliefs. This means both parents have to do their homework with each other and come up with a workable game plan (Julie and I did this even though our beliefs are mostly similar). This effort is especially critical for divorced parents, where the lines of communication and cooperation are even more complicated. It's not a good alternative to toss up our hands and let our children decide. Our children need our leadership and guidance in a few critical areas in their lives, and this is definitely one of them. We need to determine the essential moral beliefs and values of our home. We also need to share our basic religious beliefs in a way that will benefit our children. A very good resource for exploring the issue of interfaith religious education, and interfaith family life generally, is *The Interfaith Family Guidebook* by Joan C. Hawxhurst (Kalamazoo, MI: Dovetail Publishing, 1998).

When you have sorted out the united front you will present to your kids issues of faith and religion, be sure to share it with your parents and in-laws. It can be very painful for the grandparents to discover that you're raising your kids in a faith different from their own. They can unwittingly or consciously create divisiveness or confusion among your kids by "correcting" or undermining what you're teaching.

Explain to your parents and in-laws in a loving but firm way how you're choosing to raise your children, and ask them to respect any differences of religion or faith. Appreciate that any anger or indignation often springs from a sense that they have personally failed in their roles as leaders of your religious upbringing. Stress the common elements of how you were raised and how you're raising your kids. If there are specific religious practices you want them to avoid around your kids, spell them out. My friend who was raised Catholic and married a Jew decided she wanted their kids to be raised Jewish. She became exasperated when her family kept sending explicitly religious hand towels and decorations at Christmas, and was dismayed when one sibling asked whether she planned to have the children baptized "just in case." She's worked hard to educate her parents about the new traditions she celebrates with her husband and children, and was delighted when her father attended his first seder in his seventies.

Clearly, interfaith life is more difficult if your religious belief includes the notion that people who don't believe as you do will experience everlasting punishment. Your natural desire is to protect your loved ones from this very unhappy consequence. Nonetheless, you have chosen to marry someone who has a different point of view, and he or she needs your love, respect, and loyalty. You may want to influence your mate, but beyond that, you need to let go and love. There's no need to needlessly take on the role of God. It's not easy for us to sort out religious matters, and God certainly knows this. We can only hope that God is at least as wise, understanding, and loving as the most wise, understanding, and loving people we have known. By the grace of God we are here, by the grace of God we will continue to live on after we die, and by God's grace we will live on in a manner that God alone provides.

When two loving minds are united in a single purpose, there is a mighty mental force which will unfailingly accomplish the purpose.

—LEON DE SEBLO

Life As Scripture

All people can see the handiwork of God; it is all around them.
—RUMI

❧

I HAVE GREAT RESPECT FOR THE SCRIPTURE AND SACRED TEXTS of Judaism, Christianity, and the other world religions. I have seen the lives of friends changed and benefited as they have anchored their lives to sacred writings like the Bible. I also have high regard for the beneficial writings of novelists, poets, philosophers, and others who have been inspired to share their wisdom and inspiration with the rest of us. For me, scripture is whatever reveals God and life to us and gives us comfort, inspiration, and guidance. I believe that different books, and even different passages and pages, become scripture for different people. Although not all the writings and stories found in traditionally sacred books are consistent with my own views of God, life, and happiness, I have been able to extract valuable ideas that benefit my life. As helpful as all of these writings are, however, they are not God.

I'm not only humbled and awestruck by the magnitude, scale, and beauty of God's creation, I'm always surprised at the things we can learn about God through life. Sometimes we can go through life reading and hearing about God but being oblivious to His great work—life. It is critical to our children's spiritual well-being that we help them to be aware of, learn from, and have reverence for God's gift of life.

Regardless of the level of inspiration (or lack thereof) of those

who have written sacred texts, people
of faith can depend upon life itself
as the direct manuscript of God.
Up until the sixteenth century, there
was no English version of the Bible,
and most English-speaking common

> Life, the direct word
> of God, remains the
> most fundamental of
> "sacred texts."

people could not read. Yet as long as modern humans have been
upon the earth, before written language and earlier, this mortal
life and the wisdom that comes to our own hearts, which family
groups have passed on from one generation to the next, have
always been available as "scripture." While temples, cathedrals,
and other sacred buildings are wonderful places of worship, nothing can testify to God's greatness like life itself.

For me, life testifies to the following:

- There is design in the universe, for everywhere we look,
  we see design.
- For such a magnificently designed universe to be in place
  for self-conscious beings who participate in mind, life
  must be important; we must be valued.
- People are born as good as any other creation on the
  planet, and except for those who become truly evil and
  dangerous—who have harmful tendencies that develop
  into ongoing evil intent—we remain a fundamentally
  worthwhile creation.
- Generally, God doesn't physically intervene in life.
  Tragedies happen to people every day.
- Since God usually doesn't intervene, we need to help
  ourselves and one another. Our greatest work is to
  support one another through this difficult journey.
- Pain and suffering are unavoidable parts of life, for
  here they are.
- Most of us have the spiritual capacity to cope with

suffering; most of us have the capacity to be happy and to do good.

- ■■ God has shown His hand: He doesn't allow us to suffer forever.
- ■■ God doesn't need our faith, but such faith can bring us greater spiritual well-being.

Life also teaches me that God is:

- ■■ Great (witness the fullness of the Creation)
- ■■ Powerful (as Initiator and Sustainer of the Creation)
- ■■ Intelligent (as Architect of the laws and design of nature)
- ■■ Creative (witness the diversity of the Creation)
- ■■ Patient (allowing the Creation to unfold in its own time)
- ■■ Liberating (allowing us a measure of physical and moral freedom in this life)
- ■■ Giving (sharing this abundant planet with us)
- ■■ Merciful (limiting the duration of suffering that comes by way of this life)
- ■■ Loving (providing us love itself, and the love and companionship of humans and other creatures, during our brief sojourn)

Life, the direct word of God, remains for me the most fundamental of sacred texts. If the lessons of a book contradict the lessons of life, my personal bias is to listen to life. I value the writings, stories, and experiences of holy and wise people, for they are also part of God's Creation. Such writings can provide spiritual guidance and comfort. Having our children read sacred texts can give them a feeling of God in their lives. But I do not believe in letting the writings of any single book replace the direct work and wisdom of God. By instilling in our children an appreciation and reverence for life, we instill in them a reverence for God.

His signature is the beauty of things.

—ROBINSON JEFFERS
(Twentieth-century American poet)

The Power of Example

Children have never been very good at listening to their elders, but they have never failed to imitate them.

—JAMES BALDWIN
(Twentieth-century American author)

ONE DAY, WHEN OUR OLDEST SON WAS THREE, HE NOTICED something new and strange for him—the moon was out during the daytime. He turned to his mother and said, "Mom, look, the moon is out in the day. Damn moon!" Somehow Adam had learned that when an unexpected thing happens, "damn" is one way to refer to it. I've heard kids use even more colorful words to describe unexpected events. Adam's response was cute, but it reminded me how much kids can pick up without their parents knowing it (especially from their *mothers*, as I tell Julie). Example is an amazingly powerful influence.

Nothing else in this book will make much difference if we, as parents, don't walk the walk. Not just common everyday sense but also substantial empirical research tell us that modeling plays a *significant* role in determining the behavior of children. They pick up on the beliefs we live by, not the ones we simply talk about. We sometimes blame the problem behavior of our children on everything except example. Research tells us that we can throw all the money and talk we want at children, but they end up taking their primary cues from our examples of behavior, not from our lectures.

Several years ago, a simple university experiment was conducted in a preschool setting. The preschool teacher placed two bowls of candy (Bowls A and B) on a table in front of her students. From time to time, as she talked to the class, she would take a piece of candy from Bowl A, put it in her mouth, and then remove the candy from her mouth and drop it in the wastebasket. As she went through these motions, she would say in a pleasant voice, "Oh, this candy is so good, it tastes yummy, it's the best candy ever," and so on. When she took candy from Bowl B, she would grimace and say something like "Oh, this candy is awful, it tastes terrible, it's the worst ever." Even as she said such things, she would swallow the candy from Bowl B. The children observed all of this without comment. Later in the class, the teacher offered the children candy from each bowl. Almost without exception, the children took the candy from Bowl B—the candy that the teacher had said was not good but had indeed eaten. Thus the power of example.

Beyond their innate tendencies, children learn behavior through three mechanisms: (1) conditioning (reward and punishment), (2) imitation (observing others), and (3) cognition (reasoning things through). Of the three, imitation may be the most powerful. We underestimate, in a huge way, how much our children learn by imitation. It would be impossible for parents to deliberately teach a child, step by step, all the required behaviors for living. We would never have the time to eat, sleep, and work. God has built into nature this wonderful gift that allows children to learn "on the job." Instead of having to sit down and verbally teach our children everything, we naturally provide models for many activities. When we talk, eat, and play, we provide models. When we express feelings, voice attitudes, interact with others, perform tasks, and enact our moral values, we provide models. How couples treat each other in marriage and in their roles as parents provides models. The behaviors that our surrounding culture accepts as "normal" provide models. By observing and imitating these behaviors, children become socialized into a family's and community's way of life.

Dr. Albert Bandura, of Stanford University, has spent a great deal of his prominent career conducting research in the area of modeling and imitation as part of social learning theory. He has found, in his research, that children will imitate aggressive, altruistic, helping, and stingy models. They're more likely to imitate the models of people who are prestigious, who control resources, and who are themselves rewarded. Children also learn through vicarious modeling: through their observations of which models are rewarded, which are punished, and which seemingly bad models get away with bad behavior. This connection between modeling and imitation is a central aspect of human life. This isn't a mysterious thing. As adults, we automatically do this ourselves. We notice what others do and we tend to imitate behavior that we like (fads, styles) or that which gets rewarded.

> Why does society act as though children aren't looking at what we do? What else could explain people of social prestige and honor (public officials, athletes, actors, and clergy) acting as though their personal behavior has no bearing on anyone but themselves?

So if we understand that modeling and imitation is so basic to human learning, why do we act like it's not? Why is it easy to see that small children learn so much of their behavior through imitation, yet still act as though adolescents learn right from wrong mostly through public-service announcements and lectures at school? Why does society act as though children aren't looking at what we do? What else could explain people of social prestige and honor (public officials, athletes, actors, and clergy) acting as though their personal behavior has no bearing on anyone but themselves? How else can we explain the general lack of concern over children watching, over and over, vicarious examples of violence and sex on TV and in the movies? What else could explain the willingness of some parents to behave badly or recklessly, without regard for the cost to marriage and family? We can't expect our children to "just say no" if we're not willing to.

We have all known exemplary parents who have willfully changed their behavior in order to be a positive influence on their children. I know a man who gave up a serious alcohol habit (something he had picked up in the Korean War) in order to be a better father and example to his daughters. His decision, and his many fine qualities, contributed to a wonderful family. Through my experience as a Mormon missionary in inner-city Chicago, I came to know a young man who had been involved in burglary and drug use, who had received a felony for drug dealing and had come close to killing a man. One day he decided to change. He made a choice to abandon these harmful ways not only to benefit himself but also to benefit his younger brother's life. Beyond these visible behavior changes are the smaller yet important and difficult changes in example that all parents face—changes toward greater patience and compassion. It's not easy, but we can all benefit the world by giving children the gift of our positive example.

TV and Movies (Vicarious Modeling)

Imagine for a moment our parent-ancestors sitting around the tribal fire at night. Imagine that instead of telling their children the simple moral tales that passed along tribal traditions, they began telling stories that were unusually violent and sexual in nature. Imagine that in addition to telling these stories, every so often they showed drawings that portrayed violent and sexual activity. Take this a step further and imagine that these parents hired a member of the tribe to entertain the children with stories that included things the parents didn't approve of. Most of us would agree that such a tribe had gone beyond the pale. Unfortunately, this is our tribe, and we *have* gone beyond the pale. We allow our children to regularly view and hear stories that would have been unthinkable for parents of the past. As a culture, we can say all we want about staying away from drugs, violence, and teen sex, but as long as our adult world models something else, our children will be inclined to imitate what they see.

In our modern world, the tribal elders no longer tell the stories, the court minstrels no longer tell the stories, the Church no longer tells the stories, and sometimes the parents no longer tell the stories. Hollywood tells the stories that most children see and hear, and too often these stories aren't the ones we want for our kids. We need to understand that our current global culture is strongly influenced by the mass media, which includes the entertainment industry and advertising interests. A secular, commercial entertainment industry isn't in business to pass along moral traditions, it's in business to make money. If moral tales make money, they might make those tales. If stories involving violence and sex make money, they will make those tales. And beyond money, they may want to present stories designed purely to expand their craft or represent their own unique beliefs and moral codes—all of which may have nothing to do with the stories we want our children to view.

Strong evidence suggests that vicarious modeling affects people, for both good and bad. But whether or not TV and movie violence turns children to violence, is it good for the soul of our homes and society to use it as a form of entertainment? Was it worthwhile for the ancient Romans to make a caricature out of cruelty and turn violent acts into "games"? Is it wise to bring the "coliseum" into our homes? Likewise, as wonderful as sex is, is it good for the soul of our society and home life to center so much entertainment on sexual innuendo and activity? By making an obsessive caricature out of sex, and sometimes presenting it in degrading ways or as the natural province of very young adults, aren't we robbing our children of their brief time of natural, childhood innocence?

In a free society, the government can't constitutionally control all aspects of entertainment, though the government and entertainment industry need to be pushed to do more to protect children, and we as parents can vote with our wallets. It's up to us as parents to assert leadership in the home by establishing and maintaining strong expectations when it comes to the type of TV programs, movies, and music that we allow our children to watch and listen to. With access to television so easy and prevalent, it's up to us to maintain the traditional separation between adult and child entertainment—just as cultures of the past have done.

> **Example isn't the main thing in influencing others.**
> **It is the only thing.**
> —ALBERT SCHWEITZER
> (European theologian and doctor)

Parental Leadership

A child is born to you so that you can prepare him
to face time unto eternity.

—YOGI BHAJAN
(Indian spiritual leader)

ONE OF THE DRAWBACKS OF OUR INSTITUTIONALIZED WORLD is that it blinds us to our responsibilities as parents. When people lived in small tribes, parents needed to take responsibility for the training of their children; who else would? Beyond providing for their family's sustenance, what was more important for tribal parents than preparing their children for their own survival? A great deal of time had to be spent in teaching boys how to hunt and provide shelter and in teaching girls how to provide shelter, gather and prepare food, and care for children. Time also had to be spent in teaching children right and wrong, and the traditions (religious and otherwise) of the tribe's ancestors.

While the traditional roles of men and women have changed for many cultures and people in our modern world, the mentoring and training needs of children have not. In fact, in a world that has become so complicated (so many choices), so technical and niche-oriented (greater division of labor), so much less socially supportive (less extended family and "tribe" available), so much less economically supportive (less employer commitment and commercial "tribe"), it can be argued that the mentoring and training needs of children are much greater now. The irony is that with the development of social and economic institutions, we've been lulled into passing on much of the effort to deal with our children's training and general well-being to others. Schools, religious institutions, day-care centers, sports leagues, and government agencies have developed for practical purposes, and many of them can play a helpful, supportive role. But if we're not careful, we can relinquish our role as parents entirely to these institutions, sometimes to the detriment of our children. As difficult as it is to find the time, our modern world requires that each of us become an actively engaged modern parent—a mentoring parent-guide.

Parental leadership in the home doesn't mean autocratic control; it means planning how to best prepare our children for life and seeing those plans through. Somebody has to be a guide, protector, and advocate for our children. Somebody has to take charge. Institutions work in shifts. They have our children momentarily, then move on to the next shift of children. They can't really love them and care about them in the same way. We need to periodically remind ourselves that institutions exist for us, not vice versa. Our children need personal managers to see that institutional support is doing what we want. Our children need mentors who will help them plan out and implement the processes that will prepare them for life. They also need mentors to teach them about God, about right and wrong, and about happiness.

> Parental leadership in the home doesn't mean autocratic control; it means planning how to best prepare our children for life and seeing those plans through.

Sometimes we need to take a stand against harmful cultural influences. The culture (accepted norms, customs, and values) of a society can be very powerful. White children born into the deep South during the time of slavery weren't born with an innate desire to enslave other people, but their culture taught them that such behavior was allowable. Protestant and Catholic children born into Northern Ireland during that region's worst periods of violence weren't born with a desire to commit violence against someone of another faith, but their culture taught them that vengeful acts of violence were justifiable. American children today are being taught through the media and other channels that violence is a normal way of life—even though statistically it's not—and that casual sex is acceptable. Is there any wonder that we have had increasing problems in these two areas with teens? As Morrie Schwartz is quoted as saying in Mitch Albom's wonderful little book *Tuesdays with Morrie*, "Every society has its own problems. The way to do it, I think, isn't to run away. You have to work at creating your own culture." And again, "you have to be strong enough to say if the culture doesn't work, don't buy it." In our culture, women are still taught that they need to be thin, and men (and now women) are taught that they need to be rich. Teens are being taught that casual sex is okay and that violence and extreme vulgarities are comical. To create an independent family culture requires personal leadership. We can't control our whole society, but we also don't need to passively accept whatever it dishes out to our children. We can engage in "guerrilla parenting" by tenaciously maintaining our own beneficial values regardless of what happens in society at large.

In our own family, we do this in part by controlling the influence of television, a major purveyor of cultural values. Before we had children Julie and I did not have a television for several years. While we have brought some of the fun of television into our children's lives, we have done so in a limited way. We maintain rules on what our children can watch, and by choosing to not subscribe to cable TV, we limit the number of available channels. Since prime-time TV programs aren't as child-oriented as they used to be (and since not having cable puts a natural constraint on viewing options), more often than not, our children will watch an old video or not watch TV at all. I admire people like Wayne Muller (author of the book *Sabbath*) who have taken this a step further and turn off the telephone, television, and everything else after a certain time each day, then make that a special time to spend together as a family, playing games, reading together, and doing other family-based activities. Not only are such people reducing the potential negative impact of television, they're spending great time together as a family.

The ultimate intent of this book is to provide resources to help you provide spiritual and moral mentoring to your children. But we need to become mentors in other important areas as well. This doesn't mean that we have to be the primary teacher or expert in all aspects of their lives—we can't possibly be specialists in every area. But we need to be the generalists who take the time to think through their needs and see that those needs are thought-fully and carefully met.

None of us are perfect parents. We don't need to be. After we have done what we can to protect, love, and teach our children, we need to let go and not worry about it. We have to be careful that parental leadership doesn't degenerate into a desire to control our children's lives. For sure we should maintain the baseline rules of our homes and prohibit harmful behavior. As family leaders, we must be clearly in charge. But like any good leader, we have to do so reasonably and fairly. Our children can use our influence and support, but ultimately they must be allowed to grow into their own uniqueness and to govern their own lives.

We have no power to fashion our children as suits our fancy; as they are given by God, so we must have them and love them.

—JOHANN WOLFGANG VON GOETHE
(Eighteenth-century German poet, novelist, and philosopher)

PART TWO

Specific Ways to

Teach in the Home

How to Do "Home Churching"

THE TERM HOME CHURCHING, AS I HAVE COME TO USE IT, refers to the approaches we can take to provide religious and moral training for our children within our own families. (I mean the phrase in the most inclusive sense possible; I use the word "church" as a stand-in for all religion.) As mentioned previously, some people may fulfill this responsibility solely by participating in their organized faith tradition (the gathering church), then reinforcing that commitment in the home. Other people may develop a stronger domestic-church tradition. And yet others may just try to be a good example and have informal conversations with their children from time to time.

Our own family's home-churching efforts involve both formal and informal approaches, and we prefer to keep the formal aspects pretty lean and simple. We continue to associate with organized religion, but on a limited basis. A community of faith can be a source of support and inspiration. But for me, it's also important to keep things in perspective and make sure that organizations don't replace God as our object of worship and devotion. As my father used to say (and he was certainly committed to the denomination of his youth), there are no churches in heaven. If religion becomes an issue of "our team is right and yours is wrong," we have lost our primary religious identity as God's children. By making the domestic church a central religious vehicle, it's been easier for our family not to lose sight of this identity.

The first step to home churching is to determine your own

beliefs. If they are identical to those of your organized religion, then this step is mostly taken care of for you. Your home-churching task will be to determine the best way to reinforce those beliefs in the home. If you still haven't figured out the religious and moral ideas that you want to pass on to your children, then you need to do some homework. Determine with your partner the beliefs that you can teach in unity (or figure out your own personal beliefs if you're a single parent). This won't happen unless you make a conscious effort to sit down and talk things though. It's critical to develop some harmony and clarity on these core concepts. If you struggle with them, try starting off with a few simple ideas like teaching your children that a power greater than us is behind the universe (this is certainly true no matter how you define that natural or spiritual power), or of the importance of being kind and honest. Once you've determined the general beliefs that you want to teach over time, then you can sit down and determine how formal or informal you want to be in passing them along. You can then find or develop the materials (illustrations, stories, devotional books, prayer books, and so forth) to help you implement your plan. (In Part Three, I've shared some of the principles that we decided we wanted to expose our own children to over time, and the appendix provides information on materials and resources that can be used to do home churching.)

Our own formal home-churching efforts have been centered around a family devotional that we have on Sundays consisting of about thirty minutes of prayer, stories, readings, and other activities. In general, we try to make Sundays a day for family (including extended family by blood or friendship), noncommercial enjoyment, rest, and spiritual refreshment. By noncommercial enjoyment, I mean we try to engage in physical and social activities that take a breather from buying. In general, we avoid shopping (that's not my idea of enjoyment anyway), we don't go to big entertainment events, we don't even go to movies. Our own deal has been to try to keep it a day that is family- and nature-oriented. We also participate in religious holidays and festivities as a family. And though we're not particularly consistent, we try to have a brief nighttime family prayer when our children go to bed.

But the most effective things we seem to do are much less formal: having conversations with our kids around the kitchen table about God, life, and happiness; maintaining mundane family rules that reinforce basic concepts of right and wrong; asking our kids to complete chores and other tasks that help them develop internal (spiritual) discipline; having them help neighbors or friends in need; and trying to maintain a home environment where they can feel a sense of emotional support and refuge. Ultimately, as we all end up figuring out while we travel through this mysterious experience called parenthood, simply loving our children and providing them with good examples and occasional firmness are much more critical to their positive development than any formal religious or moral training.

There are many approaches parents can take to provide religious and moral training within the family; I've listed some possible approaches below. This list is meant to be a menu of options, not another checklist of things that parents need to do. Maybe none of these appeals to you, and maybe a few do. Wisdom needs to be your guide in the form and amount of churching that you provide. As with all things, you need to try to find the right balance and approach that works for who you are and who your children are. There is no set formula that works for all kids. Too much churching of any type, especially the lecturing type, can turn children off. Churching can't replace a close, warm relationship with your children. It also can't replace the power of your own example.

In our own family, our children definitely like their religion in light doses, and they don't like us to moralize or lecture. For them, less is better. From the expressions I see on the faces of other children in churches, and remembering my own experience, I suspect that my kids aren't alone in their preferences.

The following is a summary of the home-churching tools described more fully in the rest of Part Two. These tools move from the less formal to the more formal.

Family Rules: Teaching basic right and wrong through establishing and maintaining rules of nonharm in the home

Family Chores: Teaching inner discipline and helpfulness through hands-on family chores

Home As Sanctuary: Maintaining a general atmosphere and attitude at home that provides a refuge from the sometimes tumultuous influences of the outside world

Informal Conversation: Seeking out opportunities to informally share our beliefs and values and answer religious questions

Prayer: Praying together from time to time

Reading: Reading good "character" books or scripture together

Videos: Viewing videos that include themes on character, positive values, and/or religious themes

Family Devotionals: Having a family get-together to read, share thoughts, pray, and teach the values and principles that are most important to you

Community Service: Seeking out opportunities for children to learn the discipline and benefit that comes from providing service to their communities

Charitable Contributions: Sharing resources with those in need as a family

Field Trips: Taking family outings to appreciate the Creation and to visit historic religious sites or the worship services of different faith traditions

Religious Holidays, Festivals: Finding ways to celebrate religious holidays within one's own family

Home "Sunday School": Replicating the idea of Sunday school within one's home or with other parents in the neighborhood

Sabbath: Devoting a day or part of a day each week to noncommercial enjoyment, rest, worship, recharging, and spiritual refreshment

Exercises

■■ As described in "Figuring Out Our Own Beliefs," take out pen and paper and list your core religious and moral beliefs. Have your mate do the same.

■■ From your lists, and subsequent discussions with each other, determine what religious and moral beliefs you want to teach in unity to your children. These core beliefs form the foundation for the teachings of your home-churching efforts.

■■ As you go through the approaches to home churching listed here, decide which would be most helpful to you. Explore and list your own ideas.

■■ Come up with a simple home-churching plan by determining the basic approaches and tools you want to use. It may be a plan that is implemented very informally and sporadically, but make sure it's given some priority and becomes part of your parenting toolbox.

■■ As you review your options, also consider the value of some type of association with an organized religion in support of your home churching. You may not be able to find a perfect match with your own personal beliefs, but find one that's just close enough. Such an association can be supportive to your teaching efforts and can provide structure to your children's religious lives. Part Four offers a listing of many of the major religious denominations and their contact numbers in the United States.

❧

Getting Ready: Determine Your Religious Parenting Style

I CREDIT MY FATHER WITH DEVELOPING MY INTEREST IN distance running. On occasion I would laugh when he would reprimand my brother and me, and before my dad could grab me, I would quickly dash for the vineyards behind our house. Though my dad was in his fifties and wasn't in great shape, that didn't stop him from chasing right after me with all his might. I was no angel, and I spent a lot of my young life running through those vineyards. But my father soon stopped chasing. I always knew if I could buy some time with him, I'd be all right—he cooled down so quickly.

My father simply was (and is) a wonderful man. Though he wasn't a naturally patient person, he developed great patience. He held strong points of view yet was the slowest person I've known to judge or condemn others. He was a devoutly religious person, but he never imposed his beliefs on his children (something he learned from his own father). While I always knew that my father had very specific, clear religious beliefs, I also knew that I could openly share my struggles, doubts, and differing points of view with him and be received with understanding, acceptance, and love no matter where my beliefs might take me. While my father would not have allowed us to do harmful things, he also gave us great latitude to be ourselves, have our own thoughts, and live our own lives. His greatest influence was through his own exceptional example and his wise and loving approach to parenting.

I have a strong bias toward my father and mother's parenting style when it comes to religion because I experienced it. Since neither my father nor my mother imposed their faith on me, there was nothing in religion for me to rebel against as a teenager. Religion for me was a vital topic that we could talk about, not a flash point of confrontation or conflict. While this entire book is centered on religion, I believe in a light touch when it comes to the actual implementation of religious and moral training. Through the examples of my parents, I have found that much of this training can be done by following up on family rules and chores, having informal conversations, providing children with opportunities to help others, and through periodic family prayer. We have added a formal family devotional to make sure things don't fall through the cracks, and simply because we enjoy it from a personal-worship perspective. But we try to keep even our devotionals moderate and light in nature.

I have seen people try to impose beliefs on their children as opposed to simply sharing and teaching those beliefs. I have seen older children who are not received or accepted in their family because they have chosen a different path from their parents and other family members. In both of these situations, I have seen outcomes that harm rather than contribute to the spiritual well-being of all involved.

Our family's approach to religious and moral education has evolved naturally as our children have grown up. When our children were younger, being more formal was somewhat easier. We could sit down and read simple picture books with them or tell them simple stories. We could pray with them without them being self-conscious. As our children have begun the transition into adolescence, we have had to relate to them on a different basis—as fledgling adults. They now take part in our family devotionals as readers and full participants in their own right. They're more interested in real-life modern stories and examples that have something to do with their natural interests (sports, famous people, history, trivia). While rules and chores have remained a constant of their spiritual and moral development, and we remain firm on certain rules, we have also had to learn to let go and allow them to make more of their own choices. Generally speaking, we have had to move from more formal to less formal, from more hands-on oversight to more guiding influence.

All children grow up differently, and some are more naturally interested in religion than others. Some children have more believing or skeptical personalities by nature. As we all know, there is virtue in both traits. This is all the more reason to keep things light. Children know when you're trying to do a sales job and when you're simply sharing your heartfelt belief. If you have a doubting child, simply accept that point of view for what it is. It's valid for parents to explain their beliefs and why they have them, but it's also valid for children to have their own views. If your children are heading in a nontheistic direction, don't panic; give them your understanding and share beliefs when appropriate. Let them know that doubting leads to questions, and questions lead to answers. Make sure to figure out your own beliefs and why you have them, so that you're prepared to answer your children's questions as they come up. Most of all, while we don't need to accept bad behavior, we do need to make sure we love our children unconditionally.

Exercises

- ▪▪ Take some time to consider your own religious and moral parenting style and evaluate what works and what doesn't.
- ▪▪ Make sure you've thought through your own religious and moral beliefs and feel comfortable answering your children's basic questions.

Establishing Family Rules

MORALITY—A SENSE OF RIGHT AND WRONG—HAS TO BEGIN in the home. Establishing clear rules of right and wrong takes us from the ethereal, lofty heights of moral contemplation to the mundane world of practical moral application. This may not seem like a spiritual pursuit, but nothing can be more valuable to our inner lives than to develop the discipline not to do harm. A very fundamental way of teaching our children to refrain from harmful behavior is to set rules that prohibit such behavior and then make sure to enforce them. This is on-the-job moral training. Governments establish rules (laws) to keep people in society from harming one another, schools have rules (codes of conduct) to keep schoolchildren from harming one another, and families need rules to keep family members from harming one another and people outside the family. This not only benefits our children, it benefits society.

One of my patron saints is John Wooden, the former head basketball coach for the UCLA Bruins. Wooden helped young men prepare for both basketball and life. The wonderful thing about Wooden is that he was able to find that difficult balance between pushing his players to excel and treating them respectfully. He cared about them as human beings, not just as widgets to help him win championships. Wooden also established rules and firmly followed through on them in a respectful way. Some of his basic rules were: "Never score a basket without acknowledging a teammate"; "One word of profanity and you're done for the day"; "Treat your opponent with respect." He also maintained the unpopular rule that players couldn't have long hair or facial hair at a time when a lot of people on college campuses did.

Rick Reilly of *Sports Illustrated* offers a telling story regarding this last rule: "That drove his players bonkers. One day, All-America center Bill Walton showed up with a full beard. 'It's my right,' he insisted. Wooden asked if he believed that strongly. Walton said he did. 'That's good, Bill,' Coach said. 'I admire people who have strong beliefs and stick to them, I really do. We're going to miss you.' Walton shaved it right then and there. Now Walton calls once a week to tell Coach he loves him."

Both for the well-being of our home life and for the training of our children, we need to put some conscious thought into what the essential rules should be in the home and what the consequences will be for not keeping them. We need to follow up on these rules consistently if we want them to be effective. We also need to be on the lookout for rules that are unnecessary and burdensome.

In our own family, we have a very lean list of daily home rules, but it's one that we maintain with some rigor. We asked our children to help us come up with the consequences. Getting our kids' participation showed them we respected their opinions and sense of fairness. Our list is as follows:

Daily Family Rules

1. No mean physical contact
2. No cruel speech or profanity (or disrespectful words to adults)
3. No taking other people's things without permission
4. No lying or cheating
5. No engaging in entertainment venues that are offensive or that we've determined to be otherwise inappropriate (TV shows, movies, music, websites, computer games, or posters with gratuitous violence, sex, or vulgarity)

Consequences

1. Make up for the behavior by apologizing and trying to restore or return things to how they were (for example, replacing a broken toy, paying for something damaged, returning a "borrowed" item, getting rid of an inappropriate CD, or restating something more kindly).

2. After one warning, ten minutes with a parent in the case of mean verbal behavior (insults, rudeness), automatic time with a parent in the case of mean physical behavior. Time with a parent means that a child sits by us even when our adult friends are there. This has been pretty successful for us, since it's very hard for our kids to act up in front of other adults. Our form of time-out, when we use it, isn't to have our kids go to their bedroom but simply to separate them—usually into a room within view of us.

3. Twenty minutes with a parent if mean behavior is repeated.

4. One hour of chores if mean behavior happens a third time.

5. After a final incidence of mean behavior in the same day, remainder of day on chores and time with a parent (we have never gotten to this level).

I would be fibbing if I said that it all really works this cleanly. The gray areas of knowing who did what, when, how, and with what intent keep all of us parents off balance. I'm hardly ever an eyewitness to infractions. Listening to my children give their conflicting views on who did what to whom can easily befuddle me, and they know this. I'm pretty sure that injustice runs rampant in my household, but I'm never quite clear on when and where.

Chores didn't work as a consequence for our children when they were smaller, so we would separate them when they did unkind things. It's important to make sure our kids don't get their way when they're acting up. We need to be patient with small children, but we also need to be firm about not rewarding unruly behavior.

As simple as the above rules are, they come close to covering the basic moral elements of the Ten Commandments (not including the religious elements of those laws). It's no coincidence that most core moral codes in the world are very similar. We all know basically what things are harmful. The moral elements of the Ten Commandments, for example, are similar to the Five Precepts of Buddhism (abstain from violence, stealing, lying, sexual misconduct, and the use of intoxicants).

You need to plan a family code of conduct ahead of time so that you can immediately apply ready-made consequences when needed. The more automatic and less haphazard these consequences are, the better (even as we battle with the "who did what" dilemma). My own bias, however, is that rules should be limited to things that are really harmful (to both body *and* soul), and the consequences should be reasonable (with input from your children as to what "reasonable" might be). If you have more than ten rules on your list, it's probably too long.

If misbehavior is becoming habitual or serious, then parents need to intervene and take control of the situation. If it's a matter of having a child who is simply more spirited (intense, sensitive, and energetic), see the excellent book *Raising Your Spirited Child* by Mary Sheedy Kurcinka (New York: HarperCollins, 1991). If it's something more serious with an older child (drugs, stealing, chronic dishonesty), we need to step in and firmly manage that area of their lives for a time. When schools or businesses get in serious trouble, their time for talk and self-management have passed; they bring in outside managers to take action and turn things around. My own rule of thumb is that children should be allowed to manage themselves until they prove that they can't. And if they can't manage their own behavior in areas of harm, we need to step in and manage those areas for them until they again demonstrate that they can take control. A good resource for dealing with very serious behavioral problems is *Back in Control* by Gregory Bodenhamer (New York: Simon & Schuster, 1983) or

Before It's Too Late by Stanton Samenow (New York: Crown, 1999). If you find yourself continuing to struggle to manage your kids, consider a family therapist or psychologist.

Exercises

■■ Take out pen and paper and list the family rules that you think need to be in place to keep your children from doing harm to themselves and others.

■■ Sit down with your children to confirm the rules and help them see the need for them.

■■ With your children, determine reasonable consequences for breaking family rules.

■■ Systematically follow up on the agreed-to consequences in a consistent manner.

■■ For a little while, keep the list of rules and consequences in an obvious location for quick reference (for example, on the refrigerator door).

❧

Family Chores

THIS MAY SEEM LIKE A STRANGE CATEGORY TO INCLUDE AS AN approach to home churching. But there is probably no practice better for healthy inner development than to teach the discipline to be of service to others. As mentioned previously, doing good has the win-win aspect of doing something that profits others, while at the same time helping us to develop the internal self-mastery that can result in greater internal peace and happiness.

Family chores are particularly good because we're doing service for those in our own home. By carrying out chores, we are participating not only in the benefits that come from being part of a family, but also the responsibilities. I believe that parents can make a big mistake by serving their children so much that the kids come to expect, not appreciate, such service. It's much more healthy for everyone in the family to contribute in a real way to the work of maintaining a household. Ultimately, it benefits our whole society when children learn that being part of a family (or other group) involves duties as well as benefits.

In addition the practical bonuses to the household that come from doing family chores (including cooking, washing dishes, shopping, and fixing things around the house), chores can also be a good time just to do things together. The upside is that we can show our children how to do things—we are training them to do tasks that they'll need to carry out as adults. They can also see that chores aren't as difficult as we sometimes make them out to be.

Julie has been very successful at directing household chores by simply handing out to each child brief "to-do" lists of what needs to be accomplished on a particular day. This has proven more effective for us than keeping charts. Similarly, with the input of our children, we have established formal understandings when it comes to doing daily homework (see the helpful book *Motivated Minds* by Deborah Stipek and Kathy Seal). We also have a family custom that we call "locust time," which we carry out at least once a week (usually at the end of the weekend). It started when our kids were little and we told them that we needed to swarm like locusts and pick up our things. During locust time, the whole family participates in a collective effort to put things away and straighten things up. We call for locust time whenever the house begins to look generally ragged.

Our children still grouse from time to time about whose turn it is to do the dishes (their amazingly keen, though conflicting, memories regarding who has most recently done the dishes is astounding—yet this feat of recall isn't often replicated in other areas of their lives). In cases of extreme balking, I usually end up giving them choices that can help them decide what to do, as in "You can either do the dishes, or you can do the dishes and vacuum the living room—which do you prefer?" Or "No going to see the game until all chores are done." Frankly, we sort of muddle through on the follow-up with some chores. But I remain convinced that it's a very important part of what we do as parents. Children need all the valuable lessons that are learned by physically participating in the responsibilities and duties of being part of a family group.

Here's a list of some of the chores we've asked our children to participate in over time (not including the everyday "chore" of homework):

- Washing dishes
- Vacuuming the house
- Cleaning windows

- Consistently cleaning their rooms
- Watering plants
- Mowing the lawn
- Weeding the yard
- Taking out the garbage
- Returning something to the store
- Walking and feeding the dog
- Trimming bushes
- Running errands

We have made the conscious decision not to pay an allowance for doing these chores. Probably because of the way we were both raised, we feel that our children should carry out these household tasks as part of their cooperative contribution to our family—not in exchange for money.

In our fairly affluent society, there is a tendency to hire out all manual labor rather than have our children do some of it. I believe this is a mistake, both in helping our children develop discipline and perseverance, and in helping them to appreciate the hard work that others do to provide manual labor in our society. Chores help our children learn to sacrifice on behalf of others, and represent a natural way to train them without lectures and books.

Exercises

- Make a list of family chores that need to be done on a daily, weekly, monthly, or seasonal basis and that would be good for your children to do for their long-term development. Younger kids necessarily need simpler tasks. "Cleaning your room" for a four-year-old might mean picking up toys and putting dirty clothes in the hamper. Older kids can do deeper cleaning. A younger child might pick up sticks in the yard that an older child is preparing to mow.

- During the week (or weekend), make assignments and follow up on them. Make sure your child understands the chore and what constitutes a good job.
- When you can, do some chores side by side with your child. This makes it easier, since you're teaching how to do the chore by example, and it can be a good way to spend time together.

Home As Sanctuary

AS PARENTS, WE NEED TO SET THE TONE FOR OUR HOME LIFE. If we choose, our home can be a positive sanctuary that contributes to our children's spiritual well-being. It can be a place of security, peacefulness, and refuge from some of the tumultuous aspects of the outside world.

In the book *The Power of Prayer*, Sue Bender tells of the first time she entered an Amish home and the strong feeling of warmth and peace she felt. The rooms themselves weren't unusual (though sunny, clean, and orderly), but the care and intention of the home was uniquely palpable.

> I usually walk around in an excited state, my mind racing, but after a few minutes in that Amish kitchen, I slowed down and felt calm surround me. The difference was so dramatic that I wondered if I had entered an altered state of consciousness.

For the Amish, their homes and work are important in and of themselves. Caring for their homes is part of honoring the life and land that God has given them. Their tasks of caring aren't rushed through to get to the "important" things. For them, all work is important. They do what they do with care. Part of making sure our homes become sanctuaries is taking the time to really care for our home environment in ways that make us feel warm and peaceful when we enter it.

But the most important ingredients in Amish home life, and in the home life of any family, are human warmth, emotional support, and positive spiritual influences. To truly be a sanctuary, a home needs to be filled with parental love and compassion. Our children need to find a safe place filled with understanding, acceptance, and forgiveness—a place where they're always received with open arms and hearts, no matter what.

Given the fact that we have many entertainment influences directly entering our homes (a dilemma that the Amish have escaped by not having TV, radio, or most other modern appliances in their homes), it's also critical that we deal with these influences in a conscious way. If we define spiritual well-being as happiness, peacefulness, and a desire not to do harm, then anything that affects our children's beliefs and thinking in ways that leave them chronically unhappy or wanting to do harm is a bad spiritual influence. Our children are too young to make all their choices about these influences. Neither our children nor their peers should make these decisions on behalf of the family. I believe we need to establish baseline rules about TV programs, movies, music, video games, the Internet, posters, clothing with slogans, and anything else that can affect the development of children's attitudes when they're young. These rules should be sensible, not burdensome, but they do need to exist. We have rules in the workplace on materials that are offensive, and we should maintain similar rules in our own homes.

Correspondingly, we need to proactively provide a home environment that purposely provides positive spiritual influences by way of the positive videos, books, music, paintings, magazines, games, and so forth that we bring into the home. We can include pictures, relics, and other visual symbols that reflect and reinforce our religious beliefs as part of this home environment. Some parents, especially in Catholicism and Hinduism, establish small home altars or shrines with special tablecloths, candles, pictures (of deities, holy people, and loved ones), and statuettes that are strong daily reminders of their faith tradition and of their loved ones.

Finally, we need to provide leadership on minimizing conflict in the home. It's natural to have a certain degree of conflict in families. We all have our own needs and opinions, and it's sometimes important to stand up for ourselves in strong ways. But a habit of conflict can corrode the happiness and solidarity of family life. Sometimes parents and children fight just to fight. In our own family, our three children definitely have skirmishes among themselves, but we stop them tenaciously if they get out of hand. We refuse to let one child pick on another, and we separate them from one another for a while if they can't come up with solutions to their conflicts. I believe this is vital to providing an environment of sanctuary for our children.

We also make a conscious effort to maintain a simple and warm environment. We limit TV time and try to spend some evening time together when we're all home. We've established rules about what's appropriate for our children to watch: no gratuitous sex and violence, and no R-rated movies (unless they've been edited for TV). With PG-13 movies that are borderline, we watch the videos ahead of time or with them and fast-forward through the parts that we don't think are appropriate. When our boys have complained about not watching a certain movie (*Gladiator* is a good example), I've maintained that I'm just not comfortable with it. Julie and I watched parts of *Gladiator* to see if it would be okay for our very interested boys, and I was simply stunned at the level of violence. I explained to them how violent the movie was and how it just wasn't good for us to watch. I also remind them from time to time that we've come up with rules about movies that make sense to us, and one day, when they're parents, they may see it differently, but this is our best judgment.

I personally very much believe in using a Web filter—we use CyberPatrol. I continue to be a bit surprised when I've talked to parents who don't see the need to oversee and screen what their children are taking in via videos and the Internet. Again, we readily accept rules about offensive materials in the workplace; our homes should be at least as sacred as the workplace.

Our children have fun posters and pictures in their rooms, but they're modest and harmless. While we don't maintain anything like an altar, we do keep up a few paintings and photo-graphs that remind us of the Creation and help us remember our living and departed loved ones. We do enjoy candles, and some-times, especially during the holiday seasons, we light them during our devotionals.

There are certainly days when our home seems more like a bustling Las Vegas casino than a quiet Amish kitchen (in fact, there are moments when Julie and I would like to move into that Amish kitchen). But our home is a place where we do find fun, sanctuary, and refreshment from the hustle and bustle of work and school life.

Exercises

- ■■ Take out pen and paper and list what changes you can make to turn your home into a sanctuary. A human place, for sure—but a place of security, fun, love, forgiveness, support, and positive spiritual influence.

- ■■ Take a stand and don't allow influences in your home that you believe are inappropriate for your children or offensive to your home life—whether those influences are TV pro-grams, websites, videos, music, computer games, or posters.

- ■■ Establish the rules and tone of the home. While it's healthy to allow your children to participate in the decision-making, it's not healthy to run things as a complete democracy. We want our children's input, but as parents, we need to be the family leaders who make the final decisions when it comes to what we allow in our homes, by way of either behavior or influences.

- ■■ Show leadership in reducing home conflict by providing examples of good problem-solving skills and by separating children before conflict gets out of control.

Informal Conversations

❧

FOR SOME PARENTS, TALKING FORMALLY ABOUT RELIGION AND moral values with children isn't a natural, comfortable thing to do, especially if they've never done it. Sometimes we have to break through our comfort zones. On occasion we simply need to have heart-to-heart talks with our kids, making them as informal as necessary, when we tell them about our love for them and about our most important beliefs in life. But we must also be realistic about our innate personalities and the relationships we have with our children. For all parents, but especially those who aren't naturally disposed to talk about religion and morals, informal conversations around the kitchen table may be the most powerful form of teaching (other than our own examples). This is much easier to do if we develop good rapport with our kids and have a good conversational relationship to begin with. When we learn to listen with understanding, to be slow to judge and lecture, and ask questions that show our interest, they will be more interested in what we have to say. But whether we have good rapport or not, it's vital that we tell them about our beliefs and feelings. Here are a few ideas on talking to our children about faith and morals:

Belief in God

▪ ▪ God is not a common topic of public discussion. For theists, God makes all things possible, but we need to be fully engaged in this life—for here we are. Many of us aren't naturally comfortable with a lot of "God talk." But since this belief is important to us, we need to somehow pass it along to our children in informal conversation. In particular, we can use life events to express our beliefs to our children. Julie and I sometimes express our appreciation for the beauty of God's creation. Just taking the time to be in nature shows our appreciation. When we're driving through the Redwoods or hiking through a fern forest, we might occasionally say something like "Isn't this a beautiful world that God has created?," but in all honesty, we're much more likely to appreciate that beauty in silence. Just being out in nature is the real lesson.

At times of death or other tragedy, we can express beliefs about God and eternity to our children to help give them a larger perspective. When the tragedies of the World Trade Center and Columbine happened and news interviews brought up the idea of God sparing this person or that one, Julie and I talked with our kids about how there were many people of faith who died in those tragic events, and God loved them all. We emphasized our belief that God didn't make this happen or pick and choose who would survive. We reminded our children that life is full of good and bad with much natural and human freedom.

When my father died, we spent time talking about our love for him and of our own belief that he was with God and we would see him before too long—that although life can sometimes be very sad and difficult, that the sadness doesn't last forever.

We remind our children from time to time that having them in the family is the best gift that God could have given us. In addition, if news items or TV programs about religion happen to come up, either positive or negative, we occasionally reinforce our own beliefs and how they relate to the news. We also sometimes discuss newspaper or magazine articles that illustrate points that we think are valuable with respect to our beliefs about God.

Right and Wrong

■ ■ Whether we like it or not, we informally teach our children about right and wrong all the time by what we do and say. When children see and hear how we treat others, how honest we are, what we watch on TV, what music we listen to, and how we treat *them*, they're getting our real-life views on right and wrong. When they hear what we criticize, the opinions we express after we read the newspaper, our attitudes and judgments about people and the everyday events of life, they learn about our moral beliefs. When we follow through (or don't follow through) on family rules, we communicate our views on good and bad behavior in a powerful way. From time to time we need to consciously assess our deeds, words, and family rules and make sure they convey the beliefs that we want our children to adopt. We especially need to assess what beliefs we're conveying to our children about themselves by the type of criticism we give them and by the amount of respect, honor, and interest we show in them.

■ ■ Beyond the moral education that we provide in everyday living, we can also engage our children in more conscious informal conversations to ensure that we clearly and directly state our views on right and wrong. In my family, we sometimes do this by using topics that come up in the news as examples of good (or bad) behavior. If a public figure is caught in dishonesty, we might explain the serious damage that can be done when people in such positions don't uphold an office with integrity. If an athlete is in trouble with drugs, we might point out the serious harm that taking drugs brings to people's lives. As baseball player Darryl Strawberry keeps going through his drug problems, we've commented about what a great athlete he was and how hard it is even for someone as talented and dedicated as he is to get over drugs. When Bill Clinton was going through his "problem," Julie and I were quite blunt in explaining to our kids how important it was for people of high office to be honest and for married people to be faithful to each other (Bill forced all of us into more discussions on more topics than we would have preferred).

One ongoing joke that I have with my kids is that every time we drive past San Quentin Prison as we pull onto the Richmond–San Rafael Bridge in the North Bay Area, I announce with a stern voice and straight face, "Now, kids, I don't want to have to come and visit you in there when you're older." When we pass a group of teenagers who look like gang members, I do the same thing by saying, "Now, kids, I don't want to see you hanging out with those guys." My humor is known to be pretty dry, so they always laugh when I start off a line with "Now, kids . . ."

While our children can usually pick up our cues on how we feel about moral issues, occasionally talking those views through can help clarify our beliefs for them.

■■ Once again, it's important to figure out our core beliefs about right and wrong that we want to teach, so that we can look for opportunities to talk informally about them. As adults, we've probably already figured out for ourselves what we consider to be good and bad behavior. When it comes to how we treat others, our children ought to be taught at least the social virtues of kindness and honesty: that we don't harm others or their property, that we help those in need, and that we tell others the truth. We also live in an age when passing along our moral beliefs about drugs and sex in clear, direct ways is particularly important.

Exercises

■■ Every so often, just tell your children informally how much you love them and what a great blessing from God they are in your life.

■■ Look for opportunities—when you're out in nature, when someone close to your family dies, or when you need to reassure your children of their own worth—to tell them about your own beliefs about God and the Creation.

■■ Use news items as an opportunity to informally but directly confirm your beliefs about harmful behavior.

■■ Use enforcement of family rules as an informal way to confirm your beliefs about harmful behavior.

❧

Answering "Thorny" Questions

❧

As much as you can try to "stage" the opportunity to discuss religious and moral issues with your kids, most of the time you'll find yourself on the hot seat when your child pops some question out of the blue. Typically, you're behind the wheel, a million things on your mind, when suddenly your daughter says, "I was playing with Margaret today, and she says that we're going to hell because we're Jewish," or your son comes out with "You said lying was wrong, but I heard you tell your boss that you were sick, even though you weren't. Was that okay?" Although I haven't always been prepared to answer my children's questions, I've always liked being asked, because it tells me that they're thinking, and it forces me to think, too. It also opens up a natural way to talk about religious and moral themes that are most meaningful to my kids at that time in their lives.

We all come from different cultural, religious, and social backgrounds. Our belief systems are based on our inherent makeup, our life experience, our personal biases, and what we've learned over time. We therefore have unique answers to religious questions. While I'm no expert in the field of answering children's religious questions, especially the thorny type, I do think there are a few basic principles that can help us respond to such questions:

1. As best we can, we should develop a level of rapport with our children so they feel free to ask their simple religious and moral questions, thorny or not. Thank your child for asking the question. If it's one that puzzles you, too, admit it. If you don't have an answer at the moment, you might say something like

"That's a great question. I want to think about my answer a little bit. I'll get back to you on that," then follow up after you've thought things through. There will be times when you're cross or exhausted and the last thing you feel like doing is helping unknot some complicated religious issue. But recognize it's a gift that your child trusts you enough to pose the question. Don't miss the opportunity to strengthen that bond.

2. If our children sense that certain religious topics are taboo, they may miss out on further helpful perspectives; they may also grow more skeptical if they see that their parents are unwilling to discuss basic issues in direct ways. Even if you're privately surprised by your child's question or comment ("Mom, I don't think I believe in God"), try not to show it. Try to respond instead to the feelings behind the question, or see if you can find out whether a specific incident prompted the question. Ultimately, the message you want to send is that there are no bad or stupid questions, that questioning one's faith is natural and normal, and that you are always going to be there as a nonjudgmental sounding board.

3. There's no need to take such questions personally or defensively. Our children aren't us—they're unique people who will have their own ways of thinking about things and their own approaches to making sense of life. You haven't failed if your child's beliefs aren't your own.

4. It can also be helpful to ask them about their questions and to have them express what they believe and why. They also need to understand that beliefs can change—that what they believe today may evolve as they learn new things. Some kids may feel isolated or "wrong" if their beliefs differ from those of their parents, or if they don't believe at all. Reassure your kids that they'll come to their beliefs in their own way and in their own time.

5. We don't need to have all the answers, and there's nothing wrong with telling our children that we don't have them all.

Here are some examples of thorny questions that we're sometimes forced to deal with as parents. I've taken the liberty of suggesting some possible ways to respond, but I must emphasize that there's no right or wrong answer; your answer will be unique. As a practice exercise, consider how you might respond.

"You're Christian and Mom's Jewish. Who's right?"

There are many good religions on the earth. Mom and I were raised in two different families from two different religious backgrounds. Religions were created to help us have faith in God, do good, and be happy. People often prefer different religions based on how they were raised, what beliefs make sense to them, and just their personalities. Some people believe that their religion is the only right one. In our family, we believe that there are many good religions that try their best to do what God wants. You can ask Mom and me more about the specific beliefs and traditions of our religious backgrounds anytime.

"I don't pray—I don't think it does anything."

Different things are helpful for different people. Sometimes I pray when I need comfort or strength, or when I feel grateful for life and what God has given me. Prayer sometimes brings me great peace. I don't think God needs our prayers—He'll love us no matter what. And I believe He's always there to listen to us if we do pray. Prayer is helpful and good for me. Just remember you can always pray if you need or want to.

"I told Aunt Jean that I liked the sweater she gave me even though I hate it. Is it okay to lie?"

Even though what you said might have not been exactly the truth, I wouldn't feel too bad about it. You weren't being dishonest in order to do harm, you were just trying to be kind. I've done that myself sometimes. It's still better to try to be honest, because if people find out we weren't telling the truth, then even our kindness can seem unkind to them. Let's practice together some wording you can use in the future if this kind of thing comes up again.

"Did God really part the Red Sea? Did he really kill all those people in Sodom and Gomorrah?"

Some people believe that everything in the Bible is true, and some don't. The Bible was written many years ago, and we don't know exactly who all the writers were; they were people of faith who did their best to write about God. For me, I think that there are good things in the Bible, but I don't think everything in it is true. We do know through archaeology that a lot of the Bible's basic history is true. I personally believe that God has created a natural world and doesn't intervene too much in it. So I'm not too sure about God parting the Red Sea, and for sure I don't believe that God kills His children if they don't do what He asks. Something amazing may have happened with the Red Sea and Sodom and Gomorrah, but they also may have been events caused by nature that people back then honestly thought were caused by God.

"Grandma says anyone who doesn't believe in Jesus is going to go to hell."

Different people have different religious beliefs. Some people do believe that if we don't believe in Jesus, we will go to hell. It doesn't make sense to me that God would punish His children just for a belief, but there are people we know and love who do believe this way. What makes sense to you?

"Why does God let bad things happen?"

I believe we're on the Earth to experience a natural, physical world without God's controlling intervention. If God controlled everything, we couldn't learn or choose things for ourselves—we'd be like robots. A natural world makes it possible to experience knowledge, joy, and freedom and all the miracles of our minds and bodies. But by being part of a natural world, we must also experience the hard things that come with it, like sickness, hunger, pain, and death. When really bad things happen, it's hard to understand why we have to live in a world that includes bad things. We can only trust in God that this life is important for us. And as hard as life can sometimes be, God has made it so that this life doesn't last forever. Our time in this natural world comes to an end and our spirit returns to God. Remember that God loves us and feels sad when we suffer. God has given us each other to help in times of need, and we can always pray to God and He will give us strength and comfort when bad things happen.

"Why do we have to go to church?"

In the same way that we have you go to school to get an academic education, we go to church for your religious and moral education, and because this is our way of worshiping God. I know it's not always fun, any more than school is always fun, but we think it's important.

"I don't believe in God."

We all live by faith, no matter what we believe. We're all limited in this life by our human knowledge and experience. We don't know what kind of knowledge is beyond our human experience, and we all need to sort things out the best we can. My belief in God makes sense to me and gives me strength and peace in my life. But you need to figure out your own beliefs for yourself. I value my faith in God very highly, so if you ever have questions about why I believe the way I do, just ask me.

Exercises

■ ■ Think about the rapport you've developed with your children and whether you've fostered an atmosphere in which they feel comfortable talking about religion and religious questions. If that rapport isn't there, consider sitting down and telling them that they can always feel comfortable asking any questions in this area.

■ ■ Look at your own religious questions with a fresh perspective and consider how you might answer them at this stage of your life.

■ ■ Make sure you've thought through your own religious and moral beliefs and feel comfortable answering your children's basic questions.

Family Prayer

IN OUR FAMILY, ALTHOUGH WE'RE NOT TERRIBLY CONSISTENT, we try to have a family prayer during each week. In some respects, it's the most important thing we do with our children to confirm our belief in God. Rather than talking to our children about our belief in God, we're *showing* them our belief by acknowledging God in prayer. For our family prayer, we have a member of the family say the prayer on behalf of all of us. The prayers are simple, unmemorized prayers of thanksgiving and blessing. We take turns over time. The nice thing about a night-time family prayer is that it can have a calming, bonding influence on the family while also engendering gratitude and reverence for God. Prayer is a wonderful spiritual practice. It's a grace note to the end of the day. It focuses our attention on our inner lives (the real lives that we're always living) and on God and God's world. It gives our children a spiritual tool that they can use at any time to refocus their lives and connect with God.

At our house, we keep things informal. We usually don't kneel, and if we just get silence and reverence from the kids, we're pretty darn happy. As the oldest, our son Adam naturally gives the quickest prayers. Our son Jackson has always included interesting things in his prayers. From a young age, among the things he would thank God for were: knowledge, freedom, technology, matter, the universe. He would also frequently and sincerely say, "Thanks a lot, you're a big help." And our daughter, Brooke, has always expressed very considerate prayers: remembering members of our extended family and asking God to watch out for our own family. She remembers departed loved ones in her prayers, including her cousin Katie; she'll say "Help Katie to have a good time." We try not to censor the prayers. We sometimes offer gentle encouragement, but mostly we let them come to prayer in their own way.

When I was growing up, my family seldom prayed together. Not only did the kids giggle, but my mom occasionally giggled, so my dad would just give up in disgust. You'd think that I would naturally understand this tendency, but not so. I have to confess that even after many years, my children still sometimes blurt out a laugh during our prayers (especially when one of them is saying the prayer). When we started having family prayers with our devotionals, smoke would come out of my ears when my kids would giggle, and I waited for the lightning bolt to come crashing through the ceiling of our home. It took me a while to remember what it was like to be a kid. I had to remember from my child-hood that it wasn't disrespect to the Almighty but the mirth of my other siblings and mom that got me to laughing. The same thing happens with my kids.

What I've learned over time is to finesse this situation: if I sense the lapse is just momentary, I'll patiently sit through until it stops; if the initial giggles are hardy enough that I know they're going to be hard to overcome, I'll tell the kids that I really need them to stop; I'll say the prayer myself or we'll skip it. I've learned through trial and error, probably as my dad did, that there's no need to force things if they're not coming together. Julie and I try to refrain from criticism. We want to make the occasion warm and keep the kids from resenting prayers.

My children have sometimes felt uncomfortable and self-conscious praying in a group setting, especially with extended family. When they were little, Julie was quite good at helping them by giving them a few words to say. As they've gotten older, I push them a little, but I back off if I can see they feel embar-rassed.

Saying mealtime grace is a ritual with ancient origins. The

early Romans, for example, had a family prayer and sang a family hymn before each meal. Ancient Hebrews would never eat a meal without first giving praise to God. In our case, we try to do this with our main meal on Sundays and at times of special family events. I have known families who consistently give thanks before most meals (sometimes holding hands) with very positive results. Just like meals together, this practice can have a strong bonding influence on a family's culture.

When we have mealtime grace, it's usually very simple (and often very quick). We thank God for our food and for those who have provided and prepared it. We also acknowledge our thankfulness for extended family members or friends who might be dining with us. I admire Thich Nhat Hanh, the Vietnamese Buddhist monk who, during his meals, goes much further and says an ongoing mindful prayer that gratefully remembers all the human and natural sources that have made his meal possible (sun, dirt, water, farmer, truck driver, and preparer alike), remembers those who suffer because they do not have enough food, and reminds himself of the need to alleviate their suffering whenever he can. I'm afraid my children wouldn't last through many of Thich Nhat Hanh's meals. They're more in the mode of "Thanks Lord, let's eat."

We usually say grace only once a week (at Sunday dinner) or when we have special extended family members over for dinner. The interesting thing is that Jackson has said the same things during grace that he says in regular prayers: before he gets to thanking God for the food, he'll thank God for things like technology and matter. And he's been known, once again, to end his grace with "Thanks a lot for everything, you've been a really big help." He still does this at age twelve. But mostly our kids' graces follow this basic pattern: "Dear God (Father in Heaven), thanks for this nice day, thanks for all you've given us, thanks for this food we have, bless the food that it will give us strength and nourishment, amen."

Brevity is fine. Creativity is also fine. You may choose to recite a grace from your youth or encourage your kids to come up with their own prayers. I prefer the latter approach because I've found that my kids like feeling that they're involved and that their efforts are respected.

Here are some approaches and tools to consider with respect to prayer:

Prayer Books and Hymnals

There are many prayer books and hymnals (some are listed in the appendix). Reading from these books not only brings our hearts back to God but can also provide us with inspiration and comfort. During our family devotionals, we frequently read prayers from some of the prayer books listed in the appendix (particularly from *Prayers for the Domestic Church*, *Prayers for a Planetary Pilgrim*, and *Worldwide Worship*). The advantage of such resources is that they can provide particularly eloquent and poetic ways of acknowledging and reverencing God—ways that have already been thoughtfully written out. The psalms of the Old Testament are nothing more than sacred prayers and hymns, as is much of the scripture of Hinduism. Reading a brief prayer or hymn at the end of the day can be a great way to end the day with our children.

Talking to God

Talking to God is basic to theism. Talking to God, through non-memorized prayer, is a tool that children can always carry with them wherever they are and whenever they want to express thankfulness and seek comfort from God. The basic steps (if there really are any) to simply talking to God are:

1. Addressing God
2. Giving thanks
3. Expressing concerns
4. Using "amen" or other closing at the end

Our own, nonmemorized prayers are short, and often our children end up repeating very similar things each time, but it still gets them in the mode of expressing gratitude and reverence.

Prayer Phrases

Praying doesn't need to be a long, involved process. Short prayer phrases, or "breath prayers," as Episcopal priest and author Ron DelBene calls them, can provide strength and comfort to people in their everyday lives. In Islam, "Allah is great" is one such prayer phrase. Other such phrases include: "Thank you, God"; "Give me strength"; "Help me, God"; "Forgive me, God"; "My God and my All" (Saint Francis); "Thy will be done" (Jesus).

Children can be taught that they don't need to offer elaborate, formal prayers to be praying. Oftentimes a few heartfelt words can be more powerful and helpful to them. Prayer phrases are also easier for children. Nothing needs to be memorized, and they don't have to think about all the details of what to say to God. There was no greater advocate for brief prayer than Jesus. Using such phrases can give children simple, religious grounding for their everyday lives.

Contemplative Prayer

Perhaps the most spiritual form of prayer (in the sense of being in touch with our interior life) comes from the contemplative traditions. Such traditions find form in Christianity (the monastic tradition), Buddhism (particularly Zen), Judaism (elements of the Hasidic tradition), Hinduism (yoga), and Islam (Sufism). Contemplative prayer, as Gregory the Great defined it in the sixth century, is essentially "resting in God." It's simple in concept but not necessarily easy to do.

In the book *Everything Starts from Prayer*, Mother Teresa reconfirms the value of contemplative prayer, a prayer of silence:

> We need to be alone with God in silence to be renewed and to be transformed. Silence gives a new outlook on life. In it

we are filled with the grace of God himself, which makes us do all things with joy.

It's probably not realistic to teach our children to formally pray in a silent, contemplative manner. This usually requires an adult level of consciousness. Nonetheless, the use of contemplative prayer by parents has the potential for bringing you greater peace as well as your family. And your children may be able to pick up something from your examples. Children can also be taught that informally sitting and thinking about God or appreciating God's works in silence can be a type of prayer. Here are two examples of approaches to contemplative prayer:

Centering Prayer

Centering prayer is learning to sit in still awareness and let go of everyday thoughts and worries. By practicing centering prayer, one returns to a calm spiritual state of reverence, awareness, thankfulness, and tranquillity. The basic steps for centering prayer are:

1. Sitting comfortably with your eyes closed, pay attention to a sacred word (for example, "God," "Lord," "peace," "love"), to a prayer phrase (or breath prayer), to a simple inward gaze on God, or to simple awareness of the sacredness of the present moment and of God's works.
2. When you become aware of everyday worries, thoughts, and feelings, return ever so gently to your sacred word, prayer phrase, or your awareness—resting in God and passing on to God all your burdens and cares.
3. After about twenty minutes, remain in silence with eyes closed for a few minutes.

■■ Lectio Divina is a form of centering prayer that involves reading scripture as one rests in God, or reading and listening for insight. While this process can be quite informal, the basic process in Catholic thought is to: (1) call upon the spirit of God for inspiration; (2) "listen" for ten minutes (by reading holy scripture), and (3) thank God and take a specific thought from the reading to contemplate.

■■ Thomas Keating has written helpful books that describe the philosophy and approach to centering prayer in detail. His book *Open Mind, Open Heart* is a particularly good resource.

■■ There are more and more centering-prayer groups springing up around the country. A valuable website is www.centeringprayer.com.

Mindfulness Meditation

■■ A general mode of contemplation similar to centering prayer is mindfulness meditation, which comes out of the Buddhist tradition. Mindfulness is a spiritual practice (in which we tune in to our interior life). It can be used in the context of religion or not. Mindfulness is simply paying attention nonjudgmentally, in the present moment, while letting go of worries and concerns. Formal mindfulness meditation is used to help develop awareness and calmness for use in everyday life. The practitioner pays attention to the breath or other simple points of physical focus (like walking, hearing, seeing, or simply being) and practices the gentle art of continually letting go of all other thoughts, feelings, and worries and returning to the current point of focus. Formal practitioners frequently sit in silent meditation once in the morning and evening for forty minutes each sitting. However, you can have a valuable session of mindfulness meditation in just ten or fifteen minutes.

■■ Dr. Jon Kabat-Zinn and the highly regarded Buddhist monk Thich Nhat Hanh have written some excellent books on this topic (for example, *Wherever You Go, There You Are* by Kabat-Zinn and *Peace Is Every Step* by Thich Nhat Hanh). *Seeking the*

Heart of Wisdom (Shambhala, 1987) by Joseph Goldstein and Jack Kornfield is another good resource.

■■ Parallax Press provides an array of materials and resources relating to mindfulness (800-863-5290; www.parallax.org). The Insight Meditation Society in Boston also provides helpful materials (978-355-4378; www.dharma.org).

■■ Mindfulness meditation has gone mainstream, thanks largely to the work of Jon Kabat-Zinn. Many Kaiser-Permanente health centers and other health centers now provide such training as a stress-reduction tool. This training basically follows the approach set forth in Kabat-Zinn's book *Full Catastrophe Living* (Dell, 1991).

Blessing Prayers

In times past, fathers and mothers carried out many of the religious ceremonies, including blessings and prayers, on behalf of the family. In modern times, priests of religious traditions often offer blessings to members of their tradition. We, too, can offer blessings to our children. In times when our children are in distress or need comforting, we can sit or kneel with them in prayer (or even lay our hands upon their heads, as ancient Christians would do) and offer a blessing of God.

When it's my turn to say the family prayers, I will sometimes ask for God's blessing upon my children. When each of my children were born, I participated in the Mormon lay tradition of giving each a newborn blessing, something like a christening. I appreciate the Mormon tradition in which fathers officiate over their own children's blessings and various rites of passage. In earlier times, Mormon women also more fully participated in offering formal blessings.

There's a strong tradition of parental blessings found in Judaism. Traditionally, the blessing of children is performed on Sabbath eve, on the eves of holy days, before leaving on a journey,

and before a child's wedding ceremony. The blessing is usually
given by the father, and on special occasions by the mother, to
both small and adult children, by laying the hands upon the head
of the child and pronouncing: "May God make thee like
Ephraim and Manasseh" (for boys), or "May God make thee like
Sarah, Rebekah, Rachel, and Leah" (for girls).

■■ The book *Prayers for the Domestic Church* by Edward Hays
(Forest of Peace, 1997), 1-800-659-3227, contains parental blessings and blessing prayers that parents can use in the home.

I maintain with my own kids that they should feel free to pray
for whatever they want, whether it be trivial or not. My children,
like me, have both lofty and mundane goals. What matters most
to me is that they've chosen to reach out to God for help or support. I've emphasized that prayer can bring strength and comfort.
But it's also important to explain to our children not to expect
God to answer their prayers in ways that they always want, given
that we're obviously in a world where a lot of good and bad things
happen to everyone on a fairly random basis, or at least on a basis
that looks awfully random to us mere mortals.

Exercises

■■ Teach your children the basic approaches to prayer, especially how to simply talk to God or use prayer phrases.
Praise their spontaneous, creative approaches. Go easy on
them if they balk or giggle.

■■ Try a family prayer by either reading a good prayer (note
the prayer books in the appendix) or by having a family
member talk to God on behalf of the family. Try a consistent approach (for example, say grace before dinner,
on Sunday, on special occasions), but don't abandon the
approach if you "fall off the prayer wagon."

■■ In your own life, consider contemplative prayer and
meditation, wherein you let go of your everyday

thoughts and concerns and rest in God through silence and contemplation.

- In times of need, consider giving your children a blessing prayer to give them encouragement and comfort.

Reading

IN TIMES PAST, EVENING READING OF THE CLASSICS AND scripture was a staple of home life. Since books were expensive, these works were used not only to provide religious and moral training but to help children learn how to read. There is good evidence that a child's learning experience is strengthened by evening readings with parents. For example, a 1997 study by the University of Michigan suggests that every additional hour of reading each week is associated with a half-point higher score on a child's verbal and applied-problems tests. Regular evening school reading might be supplemented with books that teach important principles of living that you want your children to learn.

Our family has brief readings during Sunday family devotionals (the resources we use are more fully described in the "Family Devotional" chapter). Over time, we have built a small collection of books that we use for these readings. Each person picks out a thought, story, prayer, hymn, or other written item and reads it. We keep an eye open for good stories or anecdotes from popular magazines or newspaper articles. A few of our best readings have come from publications like *Sports Illustrated*, because the stories provide real-life examples and illustrations that our children have interest in and like to talk about. You might start clipping such stories as you come across them and keep them in a file to draw on as needed.

My kids definitely have some favorites among the stories we've discussed:

■■ They love to hear stories about determination: that

George Washington lost almost all of his battles, that Abraham Lincoln lost almost all of his elections, and that Thomas Edison made more than nine hundred failed lightbulbs before his success—stories that illustrate the point of keeping at it.

■■ They love to hear about the lives and determination of people like Helen Keller, Jackie Robinson, and Rosa Parks.

■■ They love Jesus' parable about the lost sheep, and how a shepherd cared and sought out the single lost sheep despite the fact that he had ninety-nine others to tend.

■■ They enjoy the parables about the Good Samaritan and the Prodigal Son.

■■ They enjoy the traditional Jewish story, called "Just the Way You Like It," about the man who is taught by his rabbi, in very humorous fashion, to learn to appreciate his very small home and his very large family.

Most of the scripture of major religions was written by adults for an adult audience. If our purpose in reading is to provide religious and moral training for our children, there are many books available nowadays that may be easier for them to understand than direct scripture. And not every Bible story relays messages that all of us agree with (especially when it comes to some of the violent, heavy-handed actions attributed to God). Nonetheless, reading scripture with children can certainly return their thoughts to God and to the things of God. Reading scripture can give them a sense of peace and greater closeness to God. There are many easy-to-understand versions of scripture and scripture stories for children to read (for example, my favorite is *The Illustrated Children's Bible*, published by Harcourt Brace in 1993). A listing of scripture for the world's major religious traditions appears in the appendix.

If you're generally uncomfortable with formal training of your children, you might prefer to hand them a good novel or other book that teaches values that are important to you. Even better, with younger children, is to read the book together. *Books That*

Build Character, listed in the appendix, includes a fine bibliography of these.

Exercises

- Read with your children. Look for articles you can clip from magazines and newspapers that relate to your values.
- Every so often, read a religious book with your children, or a book that teaches a positive principle for living. Maybe do this on your family's day of religious activity, if you have one.
- Consider using a family devotional time as a time for all family members to take turns reading something good and enriching.
- If you're not interested in overtly religious literature or scripture, try to find books that tell a good moral tale or reinforce positive character traits.

Videos

THE NICE THING ABOUT VIDEOS IS THAT WE CAN CONTROL the types of movies that our children view in the home. Movies can tell stories in ways that are particularly enjoyable for children (and adults). Watching videos at home can be a fun way to spend time together as a family.

Good videos can also be a means to pass along stories that convey positive messages for living. In our family, we've established a general rule that some of the videos that we watch on Sundays (our day of rest) are videos that aren't just entertaining but also pass along something good. On other days of the week, our children can watch movies that are purely entertaining, as long as they're still appropriate with respect to violence and sex. But on Sunday, if they watch a video, we try to have them watch ones with more redeeming social value. In addition to movies, we've found that videos of past television programs, such as *The Chronicles of Narnia (BBC)*, *Little House on the Prairie*, *Hallmark Hall of Fame*, and *Anne of Green Gables* have also provided stories with good messages for our children (especially when they were young). The book *What Stories Does My Son Need?* by Michael Gurian (Putnam, 2000) provides a valuable listing of positive videos for both boys and girls. While I don't necessarily agree with all the book's recommendations, it's a good starting point. For parents who want videos with a more explicitly religious theme, many of the publishers listed in the appendix provide such videos.

There are now a number of resources to help you screen which movies are appropriate for your children (for example, www.screenit.com and www.family.org). Even some PG and PG-13 movies may not be appropriate for younger kids. We've made it a habit to talk to friends or check out these websites before we let our children view movies that we're not sure about, and our children often visit the websites themselves to see if a movie will be okay. There are also technological resources to help control what your children are able to view at home or to eliminate profanity from videos and TV programs (see www.familysafemedia .com). In our own home, we use the TV Guardian, which is an electronic device that eliminates major profanity from videos and TV programs.

Of course, it's much harder to monitor what your kids watch over at a friend's house. We really want our kids to practice their own (generally good) judgment here, but a few times, we've called the parents of sleepover friends and told them we prefer that our kids watch only PG movies. We've also practiced what the kids can say if friends want to watch an inappropriate video: "Let's watch something else" or "Let's do something else." Our kids have still seen some movies we would have preferred they hadn't. But having a standard and sticking with it have definitely helped us. When they've seen videos that we think aren't appropriate, we tell them why we don't want them to watch those kinds of movies, and we go over how they can deal with the issue more effectively if it comes up again. Clearly, we wouldn't let them have sleepovers in homes where inappropriate videos were popping up more than once. Fortunately, this hasn't been the case (or so we're led to believe).

Exercises

■ ■ Investigate and make a list of videos conveying particularly good messages that are good for the soul.

■ ■ If your children want to watch videos on your day of rest, consider having them watch those that are consistent with the spirit of the day.

- ▪▪ Consider doing a "film festival" over a few months' period: show a different video each week and have your children rate them, one to ten, on how much they like them. Think about buying the ones they like the most.
- ▪▪ Maintain standards on movies for your children. Make sure they are seeing those movies that are consistent with what you consider to be appropriate.
- ▪▪ Investigate purchasing the V-Chip or the TV Guardian— devices that control or modify what children watch (some of these products are described at www.familysafemedia.com).

Family Devotionals

OUR FAMILY HAS DEVELOPED A REGULAR TRADITION THAT HAS become very helpful to us in our home-churching efforts. Whenever we're able, we have a thirty-minute family get-together on Sundays (usually in the evening) that takes the form of a devotional.

Each person prepares a reading, a story, a thought, or some other helpful contribution. We've used some of the devotional books referred to in the appendix as resources for these readings and thoughts (some of our personal favorites have been *The Old Hermit's Almanac*, *On This Day*, *How the Children Became Stars*, and *Journey of Faith*, as well as the prayer books mentioned previously, *Prayers for the Domestic Church* and *Prayers for a Planetary Pilgrim*). We sometimes read passages from the Bible, or verses from hymnals. We have also used the time to introduce our children to the beliefs of faith traditions of other world religions (using the excellent resource *A World of Faith*). As mentioned previously, part of our home bookshelf is devoted to family devotional resources that our children can immediately turn to for their reading or story. While our children don't always enjoy the preparation (and so we sometimes help them with it), they almost always enjoy sharing their story or thought. This has been an unexpected and pleasant surprise for us.

Typically, an hour or so before our devotional, we ask our children to prepare something for it. Adam and Jackson typically get something from *The Old Hermit's Almanac* or a similar book. Brooke will often get something from a children's hymnbook or scripture storybook, or prepare a game based on what we've done before or from one of our game books. Sometimes Julie will help her find something. My favorite source is *Prayers for the Domestic Church* or *Worldwide Worship*, or a story from one of our other books. Julie also has her own stash of resources, and she is the best at cutting out interesting articles and stories that she passes on to us.

Each week a different person leads the devotional. The "leader" selects who says the prayer and chooses the order we go in—and typically my kids prefer to be the ones in charge. We sit around the coffee table in our family room. The leader asks the designated person to begin the prayer, then calls on each person in turn. Julie and I follow up on each child's presentation with a compliment and/or question, sometimes generating a mini-discussion over the point of the reading. At the end of the readings/thoughts, Brooke will often teach us a new game, or we'll play an old one. (We enjoy simple card games like Uno; *The World's Best Party Games* by Sheila Anne Barry, and *Games People Play* by Penny Warner, are good resources for more game ideas.) Quite often we finish up with Julie helping the kids make chocolate chip cookies or milk shakes. The entire reading and discussion portion of the devotional lasts about a half hour.

Several years ago, I often used my part of the devotional to talk about the basic communication skills I wrote about in *Sticks and Stones*. These were techniques I devised to help my kids deal with teasing, peer pressure, conflict, and other difficult social situations. I'd talk about one technique each time (our devotionals went a little longer then) and ask the kids to practice what they might say to other kids in a variety of situations. Since then, if I see that my kids are teasing one another too much, that the communication is not direct and respectful, or that they need to be a little more resilient, I will review one of the techniques with them for my part of the devotional. You certainly don't need to follow these same approaches, but it's worthwhile to consider using part of the devotional to strengthen your children's ability to deal effectively with the outside world, where many moral decisions are made.

As brief as they are, our devotionals have become a favorite feature of our family tradition. Not only have they provided a unique outlet for us to talk about important issues, they are an enjoyable ritual for our Sunday evenings and have brought a more spiritual focus to the close of our weekend and the beginning of a new week. They offer a chance to huddle together before we again shoot off into our various directions. The bonus has been that our children have been so receptive (the cookies, milk shakes, and games help).

There have been a few times when my kids weren't really into the idea of the devotional; they've been cranky or sulky or otherwise not enthusiastic. In this case, I gently try to persuade them to join in. To do this, I share my feelings and acknowledge how my kids feel. I might say, "I know you don't feel like it, but I need you to help me out and participate." The devotional is short enough that lack of interest hasn't been much of an issue.

On the other hand, I have a brother who never liked church or organized religion and battled with my dad over going to church. When my brother turned sixteen, my very religious father told him he was old enough to make his own choices about church. After seeing how this preserved and enhanced their relationship, I would be inclined to go in this direction if more formal religious activity ever became a big problem.

Occasionally we use the family devotional to do some scheduling and organizing. We just take out the calendar and talk about the events of the upcoming week and who needs to be where when. We've done this when we can see we've got a lot going on.

For those who are musically inclined, a devotional can also include music. One could argue, on the religious equation of things, that music is all you need. Religious songs and hymns can provide wonderful words of prayer and worship. Since we have piano players in our family (though somewhat reluctant ones), we do this from time to time. Hymnals can be purchased from many of the publishers listed in the appendix and also directly from the religious denominations listed in Part Four.

Exercises

- ▪▪ Try a family devotional and see how it goes. Keep it very simple: prayer, readings, stories, refreshments, and/or a game.
- ▪▪ Ahead of time, investigate resources from the library or bookstore that can make preparation for the devotional easier for all family members involved. Begin to set up a small "library" of resources that you like and are easy to use.
- ▪▪ Keep an eye open for interesting newspaper and magazine stories that can be used for your devotional.
- ▪▪ From time to time, use devotional time to talk about positive principles for living and religious beliefs that you think are important to convey in direct ways. Devotional time can also be a time to teach social skills, to reinforce family rules, or do some family scheduling or organizing (the latter, especially, with older children).

❧

Community Service

FOR PARENTS WHO PLACE PRIORITY ON COMMUNITY SERVICE as an important aspect of life, there isn't a better way to teach this than to help find opportunities for our children to get involved. Community service teaches our children to give back to the world, makes them aware of the needs of others (and hopefully helps them develop greater empathy as a result), and contributes to their own self-discipline. The key is to emphasize things that genuinely need to be done. Sometimes such service can be carried out in an artificial way for the sole purpose of making ourselves feel good inside. Clearly community service (or any good deed) can have the natural effect of making us feel good—not in an egotistical way but from the peace that comes from doing the right thing. But as a cross-check, we might want to assure ourselves that what we're doing is first and foremost about making a community or a person's life better (including preserving the dignity and independence of the recipients), and that we're carrying out those activities because we know that if we don't do them, they won't get done.

In our own family, we solicited community-service opportunities for our oldest son, Adam. We found a volunteer position by simply calling our local hospital. For a few hours each week, Adam has been able to provide additional service and attention to patients who might not otherwise get any. His hospital experience, which he has been doing for a year, has been very positive for his development—in both gaining empathy and learning social skills. He started during the summertime, but he's continued the work during the school year. We've built it into our schedules, and so far it's gone fine. When others ask him about it, Adam says that it's been a good thing for him. Frankly, we view this as part of his training, and we will do something similar with our other children when they get a little older.

Most communities and churches organize formal volunteer and service initiatives that can offer service opportunities for your children. Most hospitals, hospices, and rest homes provide opportunities for service; you can contact them directly. There are also many helpful nonprofit service organizations you can contact for service ideas and opportunities (for example, the American Red Cross, Habitat for Humanity, United Way of America, or the Sierra Club). Children can volunteer to help libraries, animal shelters, zoos, schools, parks, recycling centers, the community environment (planting trees, picking up litter), or participate in community education (providing public-service information on crime prevention, public services, et cetera). They can also assist people in the community who are in special need (the elderly and immobilized). A book that can help in developing community-service ideas is Linda Leeb Duper's *160 Ways to Help the World: Community Service Projects for Young People* (Facts on File, 1996). This book also has a great list of nonprofit organizations.

Exercises

- ■■ Contact your local city, churches, schools, hospitals, and nonprofit organizations to find out if they have community-service projects. Sign your children up.
- ■■ Seek out opportunities in your own neighborhood and school to do valuable things that need to be done.
- ■■ Consider committing one day each month to participate in a community-service project with your child.

Charitable Contributions

COMMUNITY SERVICE PROVIDES A RICH OPPORTUNITY FOR children to learn the importance of sharing themselves and their gifts and talents with others. By being directly engaged in such activities, they can see for themselves the needs of other people and how their direct efforts can make a difference. However, the amount of time we can commit to community service will always be limited, even if we make it a priority, because of commitments to work, school, and other obligations. But if we can't give our time, we can give our money and other material resources. And often, especially on a global basis, this is what people need most.

Helping others financially can be modeled directly in our homes. We can discuss with our children the charities to which we want to contribute. We can ask them to help us decide which causes we most want to support as a family. If we're already making contributions, it's important that our children are at least aware of whom we make contributions to, what the money is used for, and why it's important to us (so that the value of our example isn't lost). Many charitable organizations that help impoverished children provide letters from those children, often with accompanying photos, when a contribution is made. I have known parents who participate in these efforts and capitalize on the opportunity by reading the letters to their children. When we simply give a few dollars to the Salvation Army bell-ringer, we're showing our children that it's good to help out (sometimes the challenge with naturally generous kids is to keep them from freely giving to all the hand-out opportunities they come across). Additionally, if we contribute to TV-based charitable funding drives, we can have our children make the phone calls on behalf of the family.

Some families give their children allowances and ask them to set aside a certain amount, not just for higher education, but for charity or religious contributions. Children can collect this money in a jar, or put it in the collection plate at church or the tzedakah box at temple. Having kids reserve a portion of their allowance for these purposes provides an ongoing reminder that it's important to share our means with others.

Beyond direct contributions of money, there are other ways to participate in charitable giving, including food and clothing drives. Children can pick out cans of food from the kitchen pantry to donate, or go through outgrown clothes or toys to give away. When the grocery store sponsors a food drive, our children can help us pick out the food to be donated and place it in the donation bin. In my son's middle school, a food drive competition was sponsored that ended up with teens bringing in whole wagonloads of canned goods (teens love competition and schools can be quite savvy about putting that urge to good use). I know of a family who, for each of the twelve days of Christmas, anonymously gives food and gifts to needy families (as confidentially identified for them by their church).

Another example of the types of needs and opportunities that are available is the U.S. Post Office's "Operation Santa," an effort that a friend of mine actively participates in. Each year, hundreds of thousands of letters to Santa from underprivileged children pour into many post offices around the country; the vast majority of them go unanswered. Families can now go to their local post office and select a few letters that they will respond to as a "Secret Santa." If their particular post office doesn't yet have such a program, they can request that one be started. Children can help pick out gifts for the letter writers and help with the written response (of course, this wouldn't be done until your own children have the

Santa thing figured out). This type of experience can help children to develop empathy for their less-fortunate peers.

There are people around the world in great need of physical assistance. If we don't help them, maybe nobody will. We can't do it all, but we can do something. Fortunately, our contributions to our modern governments (taxes) often go toward helping people in our communities and overseas. And we should be proud that we are automatically making these often sizable and unrecognized financial contributions to others. But governments can't meet all the needs. In ancient Israel, a tithe (10 percent of one's income) was contributed by adherents of Judaism to sustain their religious community and to help the poor. There are people today who continue with the discipline of committing a tithe, or a portion thereof, to humanitarian efforts or to sustaining their religious community. Regardless of the amount or frequency of our charitable contributions, teaching our children to participate in these efforts will develop their sense of being a vital and helpful part of God's larger family.

Exercises

- ■■ Look for ways to contribute to charity as a family.
- ■■ Model charitable giving for your kids.
- ■■ Encourage your kids to donate a portion of their allowance to charity.
- ■■ Consider making donations to charity as a part of family discipline.

Field Trips

TO APPRECIATE THE WONDER OF GOD'S WORKS IS TO appreciate God. When we take our children to enjoy the out-of-doors, we are showing them the "scripture" of life. For my grandfather, riding his horse in the hills of southern Idaho was his preferred way to draw close to God. Many of us have stood in the middle of a forest or next to the ocean and felt a sense of awe and reverence that has exceeded our feelings in even the most sacred of human-built edifices. Every so often on an early Sunday morning, we'll tell our children that we're going on an outing. We might go to the ocean for a walk on the beach, play in a stream out in the country, have a picnic in the Redwoods, go for a light hike, or simply take a walk in our own neighborhood. We don't have to do anything but enjoy the refreshment of the experience, and perhaps point out from time to time the richness of the Creation.

Our favorite outing in the fall is to get up early on Sunday and go to Limantour Beach at the Point Reyes National Seashore and enjoy the full ocean experience (walking on the beach, looking for shells, doing some bird-watching and playing in the dunes) before other people have arrived. We also very much enjoy hiking in nearby state and regional parks filled with oak forests and streams.

We also go on religious "field trips" from time to time. While traveling in different parts of California, we have stopped to visit the Catholic missions along the way. Whenever we come across beautiful cathedrals or other awesome buildings, we try to visit them to expose the kids to a variety of architectural celebrations of God.

While I have personally gone to the services of many other religions, up to this point Julie and I have taken the children mostly to the services of Christian faiths. During the Christmas and Easter seasons, we have picked out different denominations for different events. We usually call ahead of time and have our children dress up a little bit in order to be respectful. We feel it's important for our children to experience the commonalities of seemingly diverse religions (both Christian and non-Christian). It's good for our children to understand and value the traditions of people of faith. As Leo Tolstoy once said, "There is a diversity of religious doctrines, but there is only one Religion."

Here are some examples of types of field trips:

Nature

- Camp-outs
- Hikes and walks
- Bicycle rides
- Picnics
- Playing outdoor games as a family
- Bird-watching trips

Religious

- Visit historic religious buildings and monuments
- Participate in the worship service of a religion other than your own
- Attend special musical presentations of local congregations
- Attend a college or seminary lecture on religion
- Learn about or participate in religious holidays (holy days)

Exercises

- On one of your upcoming weekends, take a field trip with your children.
- If you come across an interesting religious building or his-

torical site while traveling, consider stopping to investigate it with your children.

■ ■ As you see interesting religious lectures, musical presentations, or festivities in your local newspaper, propose that your family participate. In particular, consider the opportunities of special interfaith and ecumenical services, which bring many people of faith together.

Religious Holidays

THOMAS MERTON, THE CATHOLIC MONK, ACTIVIST, AND author, once stated that wherever God was being celebrated (regardless of the specific religion), he wanted to be a part of it. Religious holidays can be a very enjoyable part of a family's customs. A rich Christmas, Passover, or Easter tradition can enhance the spiritual life of children and parents alike. Children especially enjoy the goodies and fun, but if we can add spiritual elements, these seasons can also be a time of developing religious appreciation. In traditional Judaism, there is a domestic element to almost all of the many religious holidays celebrated in community. For example, the congregation's Saturday Sabbath gathering is preceded by candle lighting, blessings, and a family meal on Friday night, and followed by a gathering at the end of the Sabbath. The congregation's remembrance of Passover is likewise preceded by a special family meal in the home on Passover eve.

In our home, when key religious celebrations like Christmas, Passover, Ramadan, Hanukkah, or Easter approach, we use our family devotionals as a time to explain the meaning of such holidays. During the Christmas season, we keep an Advent wreath and light the Advent candles each week during our devotionals (using some of the family liturgy ideas found in the book *Celebrating at Home*). We attend a holiday service each Christmas Eve, eat at a favorite restaurant afterward, then read the Christmas story together. We also try to attend at least one or two religious community musical performances during the season.

There are many things you can do to celebrate religious holidays:

■■ The old staple of attending a church service for religious holidays (Christmas, Passover, Easter, Hanukkah, New Year's) and having a nice family meal afterward, solely as family or with friends, can be a very enjoyable event.

■■ Putting up decorations and relics that remind children of the religious meaning of holidays can help them move beyond the secular meanings that so often trump the deeper, original purpose of the celebration.

■■ In the traditional Jewish home, two candles are lit each Friday evening as a reverent way of inviting in the Sabbath (sometimes Christians carry out a similar tradition on Sunday mornings). Family members can take turns saying blessings as the candles are lit. One of the nice things about reserving Friday nights for a special dinner is that it eases the transition from a hectic work and school week, where family members may be catching one another only on the fly, to a more relaxed time focused on family togetherness.

■■ During family devotionals or family meals that fall near religious holidays, parents can also conduct brief liturgical messages. *Celebrating at Home* provides home-based liturgy and other ideas for home celebration of holy days throughout the Christian year (including Kwanza).

In ancient Roman homes, a family "flame" was maintained throughout the day and night as a devotion to gods and family. Sometimes in Catholic homes, candles are frequently lit as a reminder of God, saints, and family members who have gone before. You can invent your own candle-lighting tradition.

The book *Religions of the World: The Illustrated Guide to Origins, Beliefs, Traditions and Festivals* by Elizabeth Breailly, Joanne O'Brien, and Martin Palmer (Facts on File, 1997) is a great reference to understanding the traditions and festivals of the world's major living religions. Oftentimes, local newspapers will identify upcoming religious celebrations and festivities in your community.

Exercises

- Use the books mentioned above, the Internet, and other resources to do a little research to better understand the purpose and value of religious holidays and festivals. You might consider cooking the dishes associated with a holiday, making paper decorations, or reading aloud about the celebration.
- Explore and develop a few of your own family religious traditions.
- As traditional holidays approach, check your local newspaper for community opportunities to participate. Call ahead of time to ensure that visitor participation is permissible. Ask about appropriate attire (more formal? Will heads need to be covered?); timing (when does the celebration begin? It can be distracting to arrive in the middle of a service); and demeanor (what kind of behavior is expected from visitors? Should they sit quietly in back or join the throng?). It's particularly helpful if you can enlist a friend or another family to act as "tour guides" for their traditions and celebrations.

Home "Sunday School"

❦

Many of us had the experience of Sunday (or Sabbath) school as children. This is the part of a church service dedicated to teaching children religious and moral beliefs. If we're unable to find a religious denomination whose teachings are close enough to our own, we can create our own Sunday school. Having our own home Sunday school means we can determine what our children are taught. Home Sunday school can take the form of prayer, songs, stories, lessons, activities, service projects, videos, field trips, or any other tools parents want to use to teach their children. This requires more energy than Julie and I have been able to muster, and probably more formal churching than we want, but it definitely works for others.

I know a woman who organized a neighborhood Sunday school with her neighbors. While they came from different denominational backgrounds, they were able to pull together some simple, general materials and establish a regular weekly routine. Parents would take turns each week providing brief lessons, activities, and fun games.

Within Christianity, there is a growing "house church" movement where believers meet in one another's homes to worship and to study together. It's been estimated by the Gallup Institute that 40 percent of adults in the United States participate in small-group activities of one form or another (Bible study groups, adult Sunday School classes, self-help groups, special interest groups). Small-group activity has also become an avenue for providing cooperative religious instruction to children.

While Julie and I haven't done anything as formal as a home

Sunday school, as our children have gotten older, we have some-times given them brief reading assignments on Sundays to help them become more familiar with the traditional scripture of Judaism and Christianity.

In the appendix there's a list of sources for lesson and story materials. You can also contact the headquarters of the churches listed in Part Four to request information on the lesson materials of specific denominations.

Exercises

- ■ ■ If you want to provide your children with a more hands-on, detailed approach to religious instruction, consider creating your own Sunday school. Plan and prepare ahead of time.
- ■ ■ You can get help developing your curriculum by contacting the denomination(s) of your choice. The appendix also provides several resources for lesson materials.
- ■ ■ If you're really serious about this, consider forming a neigh-borhood nondenominational Sunday school—something akin to a charter school for religious education. This will allow you to share the preparation and implementation of it with other parents.

Sabbath

IN HIS BOOK *SABBATH: RESTORING THE SACRED RHYTHM OF REST*, Wayne Muller points out that in the Bible, God's act of Creation wasn't complete until the seventh day of rest. Rest is an integral part of any creative act and of our human experience. We all talk of working hard and playing hard, but we rarely brag about our ability to rest well. We reward and idolize wealthy leaders of industry, not leaders of balanced living. But living without sufficient rest is perilous to both our health and our joy. For theists, part of our rest includes resting in God. Resting the soul may be more important than resting the body. Our Sabbath can be one day, or part of a day, when we fully let go of our worries, concerns, goals, ambitions, and everything else—to simply enjoy life, remember God and the Creation, and spend time with the people we love. It's a day to unload our burdens (whether physical or emotional), stop counting, and simply let God take care of the universe. Our galaxy can somehow survive this one day without our dutiful worry and attention.

Our Western culture is highly oriented toward doing and achieving, and sometimes this ambition is blind or out of balance. People work beyond reasonable limits. Companies drive their employees to greater feats of excellence in order to please anonymous shareholders. And to what end? How much stuff do we or company shareholders really need? Who made these tenacious social and cultural rules that keep us running ever faster on our treadmills? Who decreed that our kids won't realize their full potential if their every minute isn't scheduled for lessons, practice, sports, homework, tutoring, or after-school activities. For our own good, and for the long-term happiness and general well-being of our children, we need to provide them models of rest. We need to teach them to be a little idle, to enjoy a little sloth, to experience how exhilarating a little lazing around can be. A life without rest is neither full nor healthy. If necessary, we need to figure out a way to live counter to our existing culture in order to maintain a life in balance.

Throughout the centuries, many religions have set aside a special day of the week to worship God and to rest from everyday work. Perhaps more than ever, we need a day dedicated to God, to our life of the spirit (our interior lives), to family, to rest and renewal. Maybe "keeping the Sabbath Day holy" is one of the Ten Commandments because only God's decree could have convinced people with our work ethic to take a day off.

In our own family, we try to commit to Sunday as a day of the spirit—a day of relaxation, enjoyment, special noncommercial outings, time spent with family and close friends, and a time to conduct a little home churching or participate in some aspect of the gathering church. It's also a great day for napping, talking to loved ones on the telephone, and playing board games and backyard games with our children. On Sunday, our children don't make play dates with their friends, we turn off the TV (mostly), and we suspend our usual busy routines. Sometimes we turn off the telephone for part of the day—something we learned from neighbors who do this consistently. Our kids sometimes get a little bored and can handle only so much family togetherness, so we try not to be too rigid. But as much as possible, we reserve Sunday as a day for family. This may feel forced when you first attempt it, but over time, it reaps great rewards for family and spiritual life.

If a Sabbath day isn't feasible, even a Sabbath part-day or restful Sabbath moments can be valuable. As Wayne Muller writes:

The wisdom of Sabbath time is that at a prescribed moment, it is time to stop. We cannot wait until we are finished, because we are never finished. We cannot wait until we have everything we need, because the mind is seduced by endlessly multiplying desires. We cannot wait until things slow down, because the world is moving faster and faster, and we cannot be left behind. There are always a million good reasons to keep going, and never a good reason to stop.

Exercises

- Explain to your children the meaning and value of the Sabbath as a day to remember God and the Creation, have restful enjoyment, and be together as family.

- Take an upcoming Sunday, Saturday, or other day of rest, and set it aside as a day of the spirit and family.

- For this one day (or at least part of the day), try to let go of your everyday job and commercial interests and concerns, your duties, and even your community-service efforts. Let go of your mental and physical burdens and simply enjoy being alive.

- Consider having a special leisurely Sabbath family meal: a meal that all participate in, from the preparation of natural ingredients and the cooking to eating, socializing, and clean-up.

- Try a practice that Wayne Muller recommends: put your keys, cell phone, pager, briefcase, GameBoy, Nintendo, or other major everyday distraction into a box on your day of rest to symbolize your total commitment to forgetting your cares for the day (or part of the day). Pick up the items only as you leave your time of rest and return to the "real" world.

- Also from Muller's book: try a little "Slotha Yoga" from time to time, in which you have no intention of any sort at all; you just participate in plain old uninhibited, slothful lazing around.

 Bring the refreshment of restful moments into everyday life as you're able. Keep an eye out for Sabbath moments. From time to time, just let go of everything and let God take care of the universe.

PART THREE

Scripts for Teaching

Positive Virtues

Overview

EARLY IN OUR HOME-CHURCHING EFFORTS WE MADE A LIST OF principles of living that we wanted to pass on to our children. In addition to basic rules of right and wrong, we also wanted to teach them some things that would enhance their happiness and resilience. We went through books on virtues, reviewed the positive things that we had been taught by our parents and others, as well as the traditional values taught by various religious traditions, and talked and reasoned back and forth. The scripts in this section are the end result of our efforts.

My own view is that virtues aren't virtues simply because people have defined them as such over the centuries. Virtues are principles for happy and beneficial living. It's important for each of us to rediscover, in our own time, what these principles are. This is important both for our own lives and for teaching our children. Part of our home-churching efforts can include teaching these principles to our children. My list may not be the same as yours; use them as a jumping-off place for discussion of your own values and principles.

Mostly, our family devotionals involve simple thoughts, stories, or prayer/hymnal readings that are oriented toward thanksgiving, inspiration, or comfort. Julie and I try to avoid material that is preachy. But from time to time, as we perceive a need, we sit down and talk directly with our kids about a positive principle for living. We wrote the following scripts to help us remember the basic logic and approach to talking about these principles. We generally don't use the scripts verbatim, but we do either review the script ahead of time or keep it in our lap to glance at (or read from) as we're talking. Or we might forget the script altogether and just find a story or reading that deals with the principle we want to talk about. Establishing a precedent for formal talks about principles for living has allowed us to talk more easily about tougher issues.

I've taken the liberty of sharing our own basic views on each principle. For simplicity I've used the first-person plural (we, us); if you're a single parent, please disregard that phrasing. I've also used the traditional male pronoun for God (He, Him), which you can alter to fit your preferences. The language that I've used is meant for mid-elementary-school-aged children and above. You'll want to simplify the language for younger children.

I've categorized this particular list of virtues in the following way:

Introduction
    ■■ Parental responsibility
Virtues of Faith
    ■■ Trust in God
    ■■ Reverence for life
    ■■ Prayer
Virtues of Happiness
    ■■ Self-regard
    ■■ Humility
    ■■ Optimism
    ■■ Patience
    ■■ Nonjudgment
    ■■ Determination
Virtues of Inner Strength and Protection
    ■■ Independence
    ■■ Courage
    ■■ Frugality

- Saying no to drugs
- Saying no to teen sex
- Avoiding harmful media and peer influences

Virtues of Treatment of Others

- Nonharm
- Kindness
- Honesty
- Community service

Introduction

PARENTAL RESPONSIBILITY

Note to Parents

It's good for our children to understand our parental role in training them and looking out for their welfare. Unless we make this mentor/protector/guardian responsibility clear to them, they may not understand why we make the decisions that we do. They may disagree with the decisions, but it's good for them to know that we do things because we need to fulfill our parental responsibility, not just to make life more difficult for them.

They should understand that as part of this responsibility, we must teach them about right and wrong, and we have to maintain clear rules of behavior. Over time, we'll give them more and more freedom to make choices, but sometimes they'll simply need to do things that they don't want to. From our experience, we can see and understand things that they can't.

I've found it helpful every so often to remind my children explicitly of my parental responsibility to train and protect them, especially when I need to say no to them or have them do things they don't want to. I sometimes tell them that "I really don't like to say no, or have you do things that aren't fun. It's one of the unfun things I do as a parent, but I really don't have a choice. When I chose to be a parent, I chose to take on the responsibility to protect and teach you."

Script to Introduce Parental Responsibility

The day that you were born was one of the very best days of our lives. We love you with all of our hearts and are very grateful that you're in our family. You're the best blessing that God could have given us.

When we decided to have children, we knew it would be a big job. We knew we'd have to take care of your basic needs, like food, clothing, shelter, and safety. We knew we'd want to teach you how to take care of yourself, to be happy, and to know right from wrong. We knew we'd want to teach you things about life that are very important to us, like our beliefs about God and God's Creation. Sometimes (during our family devotional) we'll talk to you directly about some of these things.

The most important things that parents have to do are to love, protect, and train their children. We've set up rules that we think are important to protect and train you—rules like not hurting others, not talking mean to others, and telling the truth. We also give you chores and responsibilities to both train you and to make sure that we're all helping out in the family. Sometimes rules and responsibilities may not be fun, and you may not like them. It's fine for you to respectfully tell us how you feel when you think we're being too hard. But a lot of times we need to stick to our decisions.

Over time, we'll have you make more and more of your own choices. This is also part of your training. But we'll always have basic family rules that need to be followed and chores that everyone needs to help with.

You can think of it kind of like Star Wars. *Obi-Wan Kenobi is responsible for protecting and training Luke and Leia. Obi-Wan asks Luke to practice, carry out chores, and follow rules so that he can become a Jedi Knight; he teaches Leia and helps protect her so she'll be able to lead her people. Sometimes we require you to do things you don't want to do because we want you to grow up a happy and successful adult.*

One of the unfun things we do as parents is to say no to you kids or get you to do things you don't want to. We don't have rules and chores to make life unfun, we have them to protect and train you.

Questions to Ask Your Kids

- Why is it important for parents to protect and train their children?
- If you were a parent, what rules would you establish to protect your children?
- What would you teach your children about right and wrong?
- What do you think would be hardest about being a parent?
- What would be the "funnest" thing about being a parent?
- What are the hardest and "funnest" things about being a kid?

Virtues of Faith

TRUST IN GOD

Note to Parents

The family of faith holds a common belief in an ultimate creative force behind the physical universe. Within this family of faith are many views of God (or that creative force). Some hold very clear and specific views of God that come from the teachings of holy books and holy people. Others are equally devout but have more general views of God that come from reason, intuition, or personal experience. Yet others have a sense that there is simply something greater behind the universe.

Whatever your views, it's important to share them with your children. Those of us who believe in God find this faith a vital source of hope and optimism throughout the course of our lives. Particularly beneficial to our happiness is to develop a trust in God—a sense that no matter what life may bring us, everything will be all right in the long run. Trusting in God means to trust in God's love and purposes, even when we don't completely understand. This type of unconditional faith can sustain and strengthen us.

Because beliefs about God are so personalized and varied, I have taken license to present my own general belief in this script. Please present your own specific views to your children.

Script to Introduce Trust in God

God is the Creator of the universe. The sun, the moon, the stars, the earth, and everything on the earth, including people, are the result of God's design.

Throughout time, people have known God by many different names. There have been many holy people and holy books that have praised and honored God. We do not see God, yet everywhere we see the wonder of His design. The setting of the sun, the sand on the beach, the falling of snow in the forest, the smile and coo of a baby all tell us that our universe has been planned and designed by a great Power. Like an architect who designs a building, God designed the laws and processes that have made the universe possible. God's design allows the miracles of nature and life to unfold.

One of those miracles is us. There's no greater honor than to be one of God's creations. We have a physical body that lets us experience the outer physical world. We also have a life inside us made up of thoughts, feelings, willpower, imagination, and memories. This part of our lives is sometimes called our soul or spirit.

By being part of this natural world, life gives us a chance to try new things, to learn, to play, to work, to laugh, to cry, to succeed, and to fail. We have an opportunity to experience all the miracles of our bodies and minds, as well as the freedom to make many of our own choices. If God controlled everything we did and everything that happened to us, we would be like robots, unable to choose or learn anything for ourselves.

But by being part of this natural world, we also experience the hard things that are part of it. In this world there is sickness, hunger, pain, and death. Both good and bad things happen to people. But the suffering and pain that we experience in this life doesn't go on forever. Our life on the earth comes to an end and our spirit returns to God.

Life also teaches us that we're meant to help one another while we're here. God doesn't appear and solve our problems. It's as though we've all been washed ashore on a huge island called Earth. Some people land on a beautiful part of the island, where they have lots of food and warm shelter. Others land where they don't even have enough to eat. Others land with a crippled body or great sickness. We must choose how we will spend our time on this island. If we land on a poor side of the island with nothing to eat, we will need to constantly search for food. If we land on a plentiful part of the island, we can enjoy our good luck. We can play on the island, learn about it, and enjoy it. But we can also choose to seek out those who are searching for food or who were crushed as they were washed ashore, and see what we can do to help them. We can choose to help others.

Having faith in God means placing our trust in God. Faith isn't believing that God will give us whatever we want if we just ask hard enough. Faith is trust in God's love and plan, even when we don't get what we want. We're here on this earth to experience a natural world, seek out happiness, and to do good. We're here for a short time, but sometimes life can be hard. Placing our trust in God can give us strength and comfort.

Questions to Ask Your Kids

- What do you think it means to trust in God?
- How can this trust help us when we go through hard times?
- What are the most important things for us to do in this world?
- How do you think God wants people to live on the earth?

REVERENCE FOR LIFE

Note to Parents

Part of having faith in God is to honor and respect God. One of the most direct ways of doing this is to honor and respect God's Creation. It's difficult to have love for God without loving and honoring the Creation. Having this honor affects how we live. If we have reverence for life, we tend to be more grateful and not to take life so much for granted. We seek to protect the earth and its resources rather than to destroy or waste them. We are more accepting and less judgmental of what happens naturally in life. A reverence for life means a reverence for other people. Reverence for life can transform our relationships with people and nature from modes of dominion to modes of kinship. As with the ancient traditions of indigenous people, reverence for life is best taught through example. When children see that we respect and honor life, that we enjoy and appreciate the natural world, they will be more likely to do the same.

Script for Introducing Reverence for Life

Life has come to us from God. The wonder of God's design is everywhere for us to see. If we pay attention, we find that ordinary things are very amazing. For example, we are so used to our body that we forget what an amazing thing it is. Our body consists of more than ten million trillion cells, all coming from one single cell. All of our cells have been designed to organize themselves (just like little worker bees). They allow us to breathe, eat, think, and play. They allow us to read books, talk to friends, ride bikes, and play sports. We have eyes that can see pictures, ears that can hear music, arms that can throw baseballs, all because of these little cells organizing themselves. Even if parts of our bodies don't work perfectly, our cells still automatically do millions of things for us each day and allow us to be here and experience life with our friends and family.

But our body is only one example. The earth is filled with mammals, birds, reptiles, mountains, oceans, rivers, lakes, forests, and deserts. Each blade of grass, piece of sand, flower, butterfly, and snowflake is an amazing creation when we stop to really notice. Our earth and the universe are amazing creations.

One important way we show love for God is by having reverence for His Creation. Reverence means showing respect and honor, and we can express it in our everyday living by respecting and honoring life itself. When we enter a forest or mountain meadow, or sit by a lake, it's good to honor and respect these beautiful works of God. It's good to help to protect the environment and keep it clean. When we deal with people, it's good to be respectful of them—even as we protect ourselves from dangerous and mean people who might do us harm. It's also good to honor and respect ourselves and the bodies and minds that we have been given.

God has created a world that provides us with our needs. God has given us life. We show reverence for God and life by being grateful for these things and by respecting and honoring God's works.

Questions to Ask Your Kids

- Do you understand what reverence for life means?
- How do we show reverence for life?
- Why is it good to help protect the environment and keep it clean?

PRAYER

Note to Parents

One of the best ways we can help our children to develop a meaningful religious life is to teach them to pray. Prayer is the essence of personal religious practice—the direct worship of and communion with God. According to recent Gallup polls, nine of ten U.S. adults say that they pray, and 97 percent of those who pray believe their prayers are heard.

My own view is that children should be taught to pray out of reverence and love, rather than out of fear or guilt. Many ancient religious rites were intended to appease the gods. Prayers and sacrifices were offered to encourage the gods to do good things and to keep them from doing bad things. This view continues in different forms today. A common view holds that if we just believe hard enough, God will give us what we want—and if we don't, all bets are off. What little credit we sometimes give to God's love!

The reality of life is that we're meant to be here. We're meant to experience this life in all its wonderful and terrible shades of natural possibilities. We can ask God for anything we want to in prayer, but ultimately we need to remember that God's purpose isn't to shield us from this life but to have us pass through it. It's natural for us to cry out for help in times of need, or to plead that we be spared from tragedy. But there's no evidence to suggest that people of faith experience accidents and tragedies any less than anybody else. Bad things happen to everyone, even to those who pray. So why pray? This is like asking why we should communicate with our loved ones if they don't always give us what we want. We communicate with our loved ones to express our thankfulness, to share joy and pain, and to seek out their understanding, sympathy, and support. Prayer offers us the opportunity to express our most intimate, unpretentious selves to God and the universe. We can certainly ask for God's blessings, and doing so for our loved ones is a wonderful way to express our love for them. But we also need to consider the possibility that, aside from the everyday blessings (and sorrows) that come from just being alive, God's direct blessings in this life may be more spiritual than physical in form.

To build our children's trust and confidence in God, we need to explain this. They will be disappointed if they view God as a genie. They will be disappointed if they think that they can just believe hard enough and God will give them whatever they ask for. And they will approach God in guilt and fear (or maybe not at all) if they believe that God responds only to the prayers of the most faithful.

As described earlier, there are many ways to pray. The best way to teach children to pray is to pray with them. But it's also important to teach them about the concept of prayer in a way that will fortify their trust in God, will not lead to disappointment, and will engender prayer practices that are based in reverence and love, rather than fear and guilt.

Script for Introducing Prayer

A good way to show honor and respect to God is to give thanks to God through prayer. We can give thanks by talking to God out loud or in our minds. Prayers don't need to be long; they can be very short. We can give thanks by using a short prayer phrase like "Thank you, God." We can also give thanks by just sitting quietly and thinking about God and His great works. But prayer can be more than giving thanks. We can also pray to God when we feel bad or need help. Just as with good friends, we can tell God about our hard times as well as our good times. The nice thing about prayer is that we can talk to God any time and any place. Always remember that God understands our pain, our fears, and our mistakes and loves us no matter what. Who else can love and understand us more than the one who created us? Whenever you're afraid or feeling bad, you can talk to God. Just talking to God can sometimes help us feel better.

You should feel free to ask God for anything you want, but remember that God doesn't always give us what we want. We're on this planet for a very short time, and we're meant to experience both the good and bad parts of a natural world. Bad things like accidents, sickness, and death can happen to anyone, even to people who pray.

Always remember that God loves and understands you. God can give you comfort when you have to go through hard things. Just saying things like "Please help me, God," or "Please make me strong, God," can be a help. It's good to pray to God when you need help and have bad times.

Just as with faith, God doesn't need our prayers. God will love you whether you pray to Him or not. Prayer is for us. It's a way for us to talk to God, to give God thanks, and to seek out God's help. We will pray sometimes as a family, but you can pray any time at all on your own.

Questions to Ask Your Kids

▪▪ How can prayer be helpful to us in our lives?
▪▪ What are different ways that people can pray?
▪▪ Do you think God always gives people whatever they ask for when they pray?

❦

Virtues of Happiness

SELF-REGARD

Note to Parents

As parents, we basically want two things for our children: to be happy, and to do good. The biggest influence on their happiness is what they believe about themselves. The most important belief we can teach them about themselves is that they are fundamentally worthwhile. The best thing we can tell them about doing good is that it is always the right thing to do. But if we carelessly mix these two beliefs, by insisting, for example, that our children are worthwhile only when they do good, we may set them up for a lifetime of turbulence and insecurity.

Children need to learn to accept the fundamental truth about themselves: that they are normal, worthwhile human beings with natural strengths and weaknesses. They need to learn that it is a normal part of being human to sometimes make mistakes, have accidents, not be liked, and go through hard times. As theists, we need to learn not only to accept and revere the Creation, but to accept ourselves as part of it. We need to work on changing any of our natural tendencies that do harm to ourselves or others. Just because tendencies are natural doesn't make them good. We need to help our children change any destructive behavior. But children also need to be reminded of the inherent worth they have as a creation of God. As Epictetus taught almost two thousand years ago:

> If a person could be persuaded of this principle as he ought, that we are all first of all children of God, and that God is the

father of gods and men, I think that he would never conceive a single abject or ignoble thought about himself.

There's no doubt that a child's chronic harmful behavior will tarnish self-regard, as it should. It's not healthy to have regard for bad behavior. If they're getting into habits of hurtful behavior, our children need to be trained and disciplined to change their ways. But there are also children who demonstrate healthy, normal human behavior and do not have the self-regard they need to be happy. These children must develop a core belief of self-worth.

In addition to our love and kindness (which contribute significantly to a child's level of self-regard), probably the most important gift that we can give our children is an ability to fend off unfounded negative beliefs about themselves. Lack of self-regard often comes from ideas that children have come to believe about themselves and the world. It's important for us to not overcriticize or condemn our children. It's important to pay attention to manifestations of self-defeating beliefs and thinking, and to help our children counter those patterns. For exercises to help children become aware of and stave off such beliefs and thoughts, please see Chapter Six—on helping children respond to self-defeating thoughts—in my previous book, *Sticks and Stones*.

Script to Introduce Self-Regard

Part of having reverence for life is having reverence for ourselves. This reverence is sometimes called self-regard. If you are here on the earth, you are a creation of God. As a creation of God, you're as good as any other creation on the planet—as good as the mountains, the rivers, the trees, the lakes, or the oceans. You also should remember that there's nothing greater than being God's creation. You could become a famous athlete, a movie star, or even president of the United States—none of this would increase the worth you already have right now as a creation of God. You're as good as anything or anybody else on the planet.

Remember that our family expects you to choose to do good in this life. We expect you not to do harmful things to yourself or others on purpose. While it's okay to make mistakes, it's important to learn from them, and it's never okay to get in the habit of doing bad things. Even though people are born good, they can develop bad character if they get in the habit of doing really bad things.

It's good to feel sorry if you've done something that has hurt you or others. And it's even better to learn from those experiences, try to make up for them, and not to do them again. But it's not good to think that you're bad if things don't go well for you. It's normal to sometimes make mistakes, have accidents, not do things perfectly, not be liked, and go through hard times. This is all a normal part of being a human, and you're a normal, wonderful human being with normal strengths and weaknesses. So if you ever have feelings that you're bad because you've made mistakes, had some accidents, don't feel liked by somebody, or any other reason, you and I need to talk about it. Remember that these things are a normal part of being a human being.

Questions to Ask Your Kids

- Do you understand what self-regard is?
- Why do you think it's important for people to have self-regard?
- What types of thoughts can keep people from having self-regard?
- What can people say to themselves to keep their self-regard when they go through hard times?

HUMILITY

Note to Parents

Humility is recognizing that while we're as good as anybody else, we're no better. But for a different time and culture, the drunken, homeless man on the street corner might have been an honored member of our tribe—a valued person with a role and a connection to others. In God's eyes, he remains a member of the Tribe.

For theists, humility is also recognizing the plain truth that we're dependent upon God for our lives and everything else in the world. Everything we have is being borrowed. When we die, we leave all of our borrowed goods behind—we only take with us our inner life.

This sense that we're no better than anyone else and that we're dependent on God, and others, leads to greater freedom and happiness. It leads, as both Christians and Buddhists have recommended, to a letting go of our strong sense of "self," and the burdens that sometimes come with that sense. Humility allows us to associate with anyone, to be taught by anyone (especially by those considered to be of a lower status), and to help and be helped by anyone. It also frees us from having to know all things, control all things, do everything perfectly, and otherwise be omniscient. It can take a lot of energy to protect our ego, to maintain a reputation, to shore up pretense, to guard against insults, and to strive to be superior to others. Arrogance is a major barrier to learning, enjoyable relationships, and trust in God.

Without a dose of humility, it will be harder for our children to find room for God and other people. It will also be harder to find peace of mind.

Script for Introducing Humility to Children

It's important to remember in life that while we're as good as anybody else, we're also no better. Remembering this is sometimes called humility. Humility also involves remembering that we're dependent on God for our lives and for everything we have. We're also dependent on many people around us.

Humility is a quality that can bring us greater happiness. Sometimes if people think that they're better than others, they don't want to be seen with certain other people, they don't want to help certain people, and they can't learn as much from other people. They may also feel like they have to do everything perfectly and look or be a certain way, so that others will think that they're better. This all requires a lot of hard work. It's much easier to just remember that since we all have the same value, we don't have to try to be seen as better than others. We can just be who we are and feel free to be with anyone else.

Discussion Questions

- Do you understand what humility is?
- Have you ever been around kids who think that they're better than everybody else? What's it like when they're acting like that?
- Why is life harder if we think we have to be better than others?
- In what ways do we depend on God and others in this life?

OPTIMISM

Note to Parents

Along with a healthy dose of self-regard, a great deal of our children's happiness is dependent on how they interpret the events of life—whether they're optimistic or pessimistic. When we're optimistic, we explain setbacks as temporary and isolated, and we don't see them as affecting our basic worth. When we're pessimistic, we explain setbacks as permanent ("It's going to last forever"), pervasive ("It's going to ruin everything"), and very personal ("It's all my fault"). Research strongly suggests that children learn optimistic or pessimistic explanatory-thinking habits from their primary caregivers—from the models that the caregivers provide, from how the children are criticized, and from how they're helped to gain perspective when things go bad.

As Dr. Martin Seligman, a specialist in the study of optimism, points out, optimism isn't so much positive thinking as it is the power of "non-negative" thinking—the ability to counter self-defeating thoughts and images. Over the past few decades, cognitive psychologists have confirmed a strong connection between thoughts and feelings. Pessimistic, helpless feelings often come from pessimistic, helpless thoughts. Much unhappiness comes not from events themselves but from how we think about and handle them. There are a few good ways we can help our children to develop optimism. We can:

1. Verbally model for them optimistic ways to think about life's events ("It's not so bad," "We'll get over it," "Everyone makes mistakes," "This is a normal part of life," and so forth)
2. Reduce our criticism, pay our children more compliments, and correct them by simply saying what we want ("I want you to stop doing that," "Please don't do that," and so forth), rather than using blaming, guilt-laden questions or statements

("How could you do that?" "What's your problem?" "You should know better")

3. Teach and practice with them tools and phrases to deal with self-defeating thoughts (problem-solving skills and "But Twists," such as ". . . but I'll get over it," ". . . but it won't last forever," ". . . but it won't be bad once I start")

4. Help them gain perspective by listening and talking things through with them when they go through bad times; family, friends, or counselors can help give us perspective when we go through hard times, and we can play this same role for our children

A good book that discusses the issue of optimism and how to teach it is *Learned Optimism: How to Change Your Mind and Life* by Dr. Martin Seligman (Pocket Books, 1998).

Script to Introduce Optimism

Part of living on this earth is to have to go through hard times sometimes. Good and bad things happen to everyone. Really bad things are death, serious illness, and not having food to eat. But our thoughts can make many other, everyday events seem a lot worse than they really are. Optimism is talking back to exaggerated, negative thoughts.

For example, when a bad event happens and a thought says, "It's going to last forever" or "It'll never go away," you can respond by saying, "I'll get over it," "It won't last forever," or "This will pass."

If a thought says, "It's going to ruin everything," you can respond by saying, "It's not really that big of a deal," "What's the worst thing that can happen?," "It's a small part of life," or "Is there something I can do to make it better?"

If a thought says, "It's all my fault," you can respond by saying, "Actually, it wasn't all my fault," "This is a normal part of life," "Everyone makes mistakes," or "I'll make up for it."

If a thought says, "This is terrible, it's way too hard," you can

respond by saying, "It's really not all that hard," "It won't kill me," "I can get through it," "I'll take it one little step at a time," or "I'll get help if I need to."

Remember that bad events are a normal part of life. It's important to try to not get down on yourself or down on life when bad things happen. If you feel really bad about something that's happened, you and I should talk about it. I've experienced bad things in life, and I've experienced unhappy feelings when bad things have happened. I know what it's like. Hopefully I can help you deal with the bad times. Part of this might be helping you to talk back to those negative thoughts that can make things seem worse than they really are. Part of it might be coming up with a good solution to your worries or problems. This is what optimism is all about.

Questions to Ask Your Kids

■■ How do we know that bad events are a normal part of life?

■■ What are the really bad events in life?

■■ What types of events seem kind of bad but aren't really that bad when you stop and think about it?

■■ Which events in your everyday life do you consider the worst?

■■ What do you say to yourself when one of those events happens?

PATIENCE

Note to Parents

Children and patience don't often go hand in hand. But patience can be one of the most important virtues to develop in order to have inner peace. Patience essentially means the ability to do things or wait for things without anger and irritation (or at least without acting out on it). It's the power of letting go.

Certainly children need to understand that there are times for impatience. If they or someone else are being treated unreasonably or unkindly, it's important that they stand up for themselves in a strong way, and that they learn to deal urgently with dangerous situations. But more often than not, the real challenge is to have patience with the more mundane irritants and challenges of everyday life.

Patience is very difficult for young children. They mostly need our love, emotional support, and occasional firmness. But over time, they must learn patience if they are to have peace in their adult lives.

Script to Introduce Patience

To have peace and happiness inside ourselves, one of the most important things we need to learn is patience. Patience is being able to do things without anger or irritation. It's trying to be calm. Sometimes we get angry or grouchy when we have to wait in a long line, when we're very hungry, or when somebody accidentally bumps into us or breaks something of ours. Patience is letting go of anger in these situations.

Anger and irritation are natural feelings that come to us all. They can be helpful to us when they get us to quickly and firmly stop people from doing hurtful or unfair things to us or others. But anger and irritation can harm our happiness and relationships with others if we have these feelings too easily or they last too long. Sometimes impatience comes from the false beliefs that life should always be easy or that we should be able to get what we want right away. This isn't how life really is. We can't always have what we want, and we all have to do things that aren't fun. If we have patience, we can still feel okay even in these situations.

We practice patience by letting go of anger and irritation when we want something or have to wait for something. All of us experience these feelings, but we also all experience letting go of thoughts. We change from thinking about one thing to thinking about another. For example, you might let go of a thought of doing homework and move to a thought of getting a snack. In another moment, you might let go of a thought about talking to a friend on the telephone and move to a thought about playing outside. In the case of patience, you let go of angry and irritated thoughts and move to more calm thoughts.

A simple tool that can help you let go of angry and irritated thoughts is called the "But Twist." When you notice an impatient thought, you use the word "but" and then respond to the thought. For example, if you're waiting in a long line for lunch and a thought comes that says, "I can't stand this, this is terrible, this is going to last forever," you could respond by saying something to yourself like "But it really won't take forever, ten minutes at the most," or "But it's really not that bad, there's no actual pain involved," or "But I can just read a book here in line and the time will go more quickly." If you're trying to do difficult homework and a thought says, "This takes too long, I can't do it, it's too hard," you could say something like "But I can take just one little step at a time," or "But I can get help if I don't understand something," or "But the quicker I do it, the quicker I won't have to think about it."

Here are some examples of common But Twists that can help:

"But I can do it."
"But it won't kill me to wait a little bit."
"But I can do something else while I wait."
"But it's really not that hard."

"But *it really won't take very long.*"

"But *I can just take one small step at a time.*"

"But *it'll be great to have done.*"

"But *I'm really just having a feeling about it—I'll just jump in and see how hard it really is.*"

Questions to Ask Your Kids

■ ■ Do you understand what patience is?

■ ■ Do you ever feel impatient? In what kinds of situations?

■ ■ When is it good to be impatient?

■ ■ When is it good to be patient?

NONJUDGMENT

Note to Parents

By nonjudgment I don't mean *no* judgment, but rather less judgment. We don't have to have opinions about everything. Sometimes it's good just to accept things for what they are without the need to assess them. As with any of the natural abilities and powers that we're endowed with as human beings, judgment is a great tool but a terrible master. When we use our natural ability to analyze things in order to make wise judgments and decisions, to choose between right and wrong, we can be richly rewarded. However, if we find ourselves continually weighing in on everything in the world, even when we don't need to, we find that our power to judge can bring us great inner turmoil. If we're not careful, out-of-control judgment can become a major feature of our internal life. Over time, a habit of strong judgment can canker an outlook and jade a perspective, which will fill our soul with anger, dislike, and unhappiness. People who are overly critical of others and of the world can often be overly critical of themselves. This harms their sense of well-being.

While our children need to be able to size up situations wisely, they should also be taught to use judgment sparingly, for its primary purpose of making decisions and choosing right from wrong. We must teach them that too much unnecessary judgment can be destructive to both our happiness and to our relationships with others.

Script to Introduce Nonjudgment

Judgment is deciding what is good or bad about something. Judgment is necessary when we need to make choices. We need to judge in order to choose right from wrong. We can't make a good choice unless we try to figure out the good and bad parts of what we're choosing. But sometimes people judge too much and too often, even when they don't need to.

We can waste a lot of time deciding what we don't like about other people, about the world, about the weather, about school, about how we look, about mistakes we've made, and many other things. Nonjudgment means not judging so much. It means to let go of thinking about what we dislike about people and the world. This doesn't mean that we have to agree with how things are in the world or that we shouldn't try to change things. But it does mean not to dwell so much on what we don't like, to simply see things as they are. It means that we let people be—trying not to talk about or criticize others too much. If we judge too much, it's hard to be happy and peaceful inside.

When we do need to judge in order to make good choices, we need to try to use wise judgment. Wise judgment means to take the time to look at all the parts of a choice. It means that we don't jump to conclusions based on how we feel at the moment. If we look at the things that are only good, or the things that are only bad, we may not make a wise decision. For example, let's say we're going to buy a new bike. We don't consider just how nice it looks, we also look at how well it rides, how much it costs, and whether people have had problems with that type of bike. If we want to go on a trip with some friends, we don't think only about how fun it would be but about how long it would take, how safe it would be, and whether it's a good time of the year to go. We need to look at both the good and bad of things when we need to make an important choice.

Questions to Ask Your Kids

- What does judging things mean?
- Why can judging too many things too often make us less happy?
- When do we need to judge?
- When don't we need to judge?

DETERMINATION

Note to Parents

Being happy and doing good require some effort. It takes effort to counter self-defeating beliefs and thoughts, to develop patience, to not judge so much, and to refrain from doing harm. Effort comes in one degree or another from determination—the will to expend effort and to accept discomfort. Determination, in combination with optimism, is probably the most fundamental predictor of success in life (where success is defined as achieving one's aspirations). Determination can beat out talent. And just as importantly, determination can ensure that talent blossoms.

Certainly determination is much better if it's guided by wisdom. The right effort is best preceded by the right aim. In our culture, we have been taught the notion that anything can be achieved by just "pulling up our bootstraps." But blind determination can prompt us to pursue things that aren't worth pursuing, or to pursue things that aren't attainable. It's not wise, for example, for people to give up their lives in pursuit of more riches when they have well exceeded their needs, especially when it involves detrimental costs to other people or to the physical environment. It's not wise for a five-foot-four, naturally slow basketball player to channel all of his raw determination toward getting into the NBA when he could achieve other valuable aims. Determining where we truly want to be heading is at least as vital as heading there.

But some level of determination, the mental commitment that precedes effort, is essential to happiness and success. Our children will not have the strength to be self-reliant and do good in the world without a measure of determination. It is not a physical power, it's an internal, spiritual power that makes so many other things possible.

Script to Introduce Determination

Determination is what pushes us to do things that need to be done even when we don't want to do them. It's not letting irritation, weakness, or fear stop us from doing things that have to get done. Many of the great things that have been done in the world have been done by people who have had great determination. For example, through determination, George Washington was able to lead his country to self-rule and freedom; Martin Luther King, Jr., was able to help bring many civil rights to African-Americans; Susan B. Anthony was able to bring voting and other rights to American women.

Sometimes there are things in life that we have to get done. We have to do them because our family or teachers need them or because other people need our help. Or we may have to do them because they can lead to something we really want—like earning money for college, becoming a good musician, or getting good grades in school. Some of those tasks take some real effort, and that's not always fun. It's normal to have thoughts that say it's too hard, or that we don't want to do it, or we can't do it. These are all "I can't" thoughts. Remember, just feeling lazy or weak doesn't mean you are lazy or weak. Different thoughts and feelings come to all of us all the time, every day of our lives. You are not any one thought or feeling. As creations of God, we are something greater than our thoughts and feelings.

One of the best ways to get things done when we have "I can't" thoughts is to let go of those thoughts and do things anyway. Another good way is to talk back to them. A tool that you can use to do this is the But Twist. We learned how to use the But Twist to talk back to impatient thoughts, and we can also use it when we need determination for things we don't want to do (refer to the But Twist discussion in the script for Patience).

Sometimes I need to help you learn determination by pushing you to get important things done. We love you no matter what you do or don't accomplish in life. Pushing you along has nothing to do with our love for you—we love you no matter what. I'll try to be respectful as I push you along, but one of my jobs as a parent is to help you to develop determination.

Questions to Ask Your Kids

- Do you understand what determination is?
- How can determination be helpful to us?
- Do you ever have "I can't" thoughts when you need to do things? In what kinds of situations?
- How can people get things done when they have "I can't" thoughts?

Virtues of Inner Strength and Self-Protection

❧

INDEPENDENCE

Note to Parents

For our children's happiness and self-protection, we must teach them the value of personal independence. For sure, children need to learn to be cooperative and kind to others. They need to understand and appreciate the interdependent nature of living in community. But it's just as important to develop personal independence—the ability to be the rulers of their own lives and to make choices independently of others.

As long as children believe that they need the approval of others to be happy, they'll be dependent on it. If they can't say no to their peers, they leave themselves open to potential harm.

Part of being independent is not automatically trusting others. Most people are trustworthy, but there are enough dangerous people in the world that it's worth teaching our children to make sure people earn their trust. Trust should not be the basis upon which our children make choices with peers and others. Choices should be based on their own merit, not as a test of trust ("What's the matter, don't you trust me?").

In interaction with our children, we can't continuously try to control their lives and destroy their assertiveness. We need rules and consequences for harmful and disrespectful behavior. But if we want to help our children to be the masters of their own souls, we need to give them room to make choices, voice opinions, and disagree—as long as it's done respectfully. The trick is to maintain behavioral expectations without destroying a child's own sovereignty. It's this very sovereignty that will give them the strength to say no and to think and act independently from the crowd when they're older and the consequences of poor choices are more dire.

Script to Introduce Independence

To be happy and protect ourselves in life, we need to think and act independently. This means that we should make our own choices and say no to other people when we need to. It's good to be kind to other people and cooperate with others, but we must also be the rulers of own lives and not just follow the crowd.

Being independent means that we make our own choices, go our own way, and do what we think is right, even if people don't like it. It's only natural to want to be liked in life, but we don't need to be liked to be happy. It's normal to encounter some people in life who don't like you. If we do what others want simply to be liked, we might end up doing things that are harmful or even dangerous.

Being independent also means that you don't automatically trust all people. Trust is believing what others tell us. Many people can be trusted. But there are also people who may be harmful, dangerous, or careless. We need to spend time with people and really get to know them well before we give them our trust. And our decisions shouldn't be based solely on trust; they should be based on both the good and bad parts of a choice. Even friends can try to have us do things that might not be smart or good.

As you've learned at school, be especially careful of adult strangers. Don't do what adult strangers say, no matter what (even if they say we asked them to have you do something); leave, and get to where there are adults or other kids that you know. Also don't give adult strangers any information at all; just leave.

To make our own choices means that we need to be able to do the following:

1. *Tell people directly what we want and how we feel (even when we might feel shy or embarrassed)*
2. *Be able to say no to anybody when we don't want to do something or feel that it's not smart or good to do something*
3. *Not make our choices based just on trust—look at both the good and bad parts of a choice, rather than relying on a friend or group of people*

We can't always control how our decisions will turn out. But we can always elect to go our own way when others try to get us to make bad choices. We can always stand up for what we think is right.

Questions to Ask Your Kids

- ■■ What does it mean to be independent?
- ■■ Why can being independent be good?
- ■■ Why is it usually not a good idea to base choices just on trust?
- ■■ Can you think of situations when it would be better for people to go with their own choices rather than the group's (are there examples in history)?
- ■■ Is it sometimes hard for you to go your own way or tell friends or other people no? What can make it easier?

COURAGE

Note to Parents

There are those who say that courage is the first of all virtues because it makes the others possible. Courage isn't lack of fear, but the willingness to do things we fear. With determination, we do things we might not want to do. With courage, we do things we're just plumb afraid to do. It's only natural and normal to have fears, and some of them can be helpful. People who have very little fear sometimes take on risks that imperil them. With some experience and training, we can also deal with fears that don't serve us well (see, for example, *Embracing the Fear* by Judith Bemis and Amr Barrada, published by Hazelden Publishing in 1994). In the meantime, courage helps us to get important things done despite fear. If we become totally immobilized by fear, we risk not being able to act in situations in which we could protect ourselves or others from major harm. We also risk missing out on opportunities and experiences that might have brought us greater joy and well-being.

Script to Introduce Courage

We all have fears in life; they're only natural. Some fears we're born with, and others we learn as we grow up. Some of these fears can be very helpful. It's important to listen to our fears when there's real danger involved. What would happen if we weren't afraid of touching fire? Of walking off a tall building? Of poisonous snakes? It's normal and okay to have some fears, but sometimes we need to get things done even when we're afraid. Doing important things we're afraid of is called courage.

Courage means different things for different people. For some, speaking or playing a musical instrument in front of other people may take courage. For others, telling the truth when they know they'll get in trouble takes courage. For most kids, standing up to a bully or saying no to other kids can take courage. For people like police officers and firemen, courage means risking their own lives in order to help people in dangerous situations. Sometimes young people have even had the courage to give up their lives in battle, in order to stop very bad leaders from doing very bad things in the world. It's natural to feel nervous and fearful in life. But these are only feelings, and we can still do things even when we feel this way. Can you think of situations in which you've felt nervous or a little afraid and you've done the thing you were afraid of anyway? How were you able to do what you needed to do? How did you feel afterward? Sometimes it's helpful to say things to yourself to get you to call up your courage. You can say things like "What's the worst thing that can happen?," "It won't kill me," "It'll be nice to have done it," or simply "It's hard, but I can still just do it."

Some of the more common fears are being afraid to speak to large groups, or fear of heights or closed spaces. It's also common for kids to be afraid to say no or to have other kids make fun of them. What are some of your fears? What do you do or tell yourself so you can still do things when you have those fears?

Remember that it's normal to feel afraid sometimes. Courage is doing things even when we're afraid. Remember also that you can always come to me and talk about any fears that you have. Never feel embarrassed, because we all feel fear sometimes—even adults. And sometimes it helps us to talk to others when we have especially strong fears.

Questions to Ask Your Kids

■ ■ Do you understand what courage is?

■ ■ Why is courage important?

■ ■ What would happen in life if we didn't have fears?

■ ■ What would happen if we didn't have courage?

FRUGALITY

Note to Parents

To live frugally is to live lightly upon the earth. This is not easy to do in our consumption-driven society. We are a commercial-oriented culture bent on producing things, convincing others to buy things, obtaining more money to buy more things, and buying more things. We're taught day in and day out from the time we're born that we're unhappy and incomplete without more stuff. We're taught that all the beautiful, happy, and fulfilled people are the ones who have something we don't. The products themselves are frequently designed to be used once and tossed away. Undoubtedly, future generations will look back upon our time and wonder why we used up so much of the earth's resources in such a short time.

Frugality is sustaining oneself economically while maintaining a reverence for life. To live frugally is to maintain a practical and wise view of what we really need. It's wanting less and living within one's income. As the Dalai Lama has said, sometimes it's better to focus on wanting what we already have rather than always wanting what we don't have. The trick is to teach children to live efficiently, with environmental conservation in mind, without becoming miserly and obsessed with the matter. It's teaching them to be both efficient and generous.

Just as poor health habits can have bad results for our kids in the long run, so can bad money habits be detrimental to their long-term well-being. Financial troubles can burden people and strain marriages and family life. Unfortunately, both the poor and the rich can spend too much of their lives thinking about money matters (the former out of necessity, the latter out of materialistic habit). There is a middle road where we tend to our reasonable needs and wants, sharing what we can and not caving in to the ongoing "big sell" of commercial interests. The Christian apostle

Paul may have been exaggerating a bit when he said that "the love of money is the root of all evil," but it certainly can be viewed as the root of a lot of wasted time and devotion. It can also be said that people and organizations sometimes do things they shouldn't be doing out of pure love of money.

Script to Introduce Frugality

To live frugally means to live lightly upon the earth. This means that we try not to want so much stuff. Not only does this help to conserve the earth's resources, but we won't need as much money to live. It's good to learn to enjoy what we already have rather than worrying about wanting what we don't have. Wanting more things doesn't bring us happiness.

We don't need to have lots of things to live on the earth and be happy. You'll need training and education to make enough money to support yourself. It's good to earn enough so you don't always have to worry about meeting your needs. But it's also good to enjoy what you have without always needing more stuff. Even very rich people can run out of money if they want too many things.

Sometimes we don't always let you have things that you want. We do this because we see that they're things that you don't really need. They also may be things that just cost too much, and we think that they're not worth the cost. As you get older, remember to be careful about buying too many things. Especially be careful about borrowing money to buy things—because sometimes it can be hard to pay money back.

Living frugally allows us to save some of our money in case we have emergencies or other future needs. Living frugally also allows us to have more resources to share with others. By living on less, we can give more to those in greater need; it's good to share some of what we have.

Questions to Ask Your Kids

■ ■ Do you understand what it means to live frugally?

- What are the things we need to have in order to live and be happy on the earth?
- Why is it important to get training and education to make enough money to support ourselves when we're older?
- Why can it become a problem if we get in the habit of wanting and buying lots of things all the time?
- How do the ads in magazines and the commercials on TV sometimes make us want more things?

SAYING NO TO DRUGS

Note to Parents

Our bodies are a gift from God. Using drugs can destroy that gift. It not only wreaks havoc on our bodies, it's also destructive to mental health and everything else in our lives. And it's destructive to society as a whole. Chronic drug use frequently leads to crime and violence. The office of National Drug Control Policy estimates that the monetary cost of illegal drug use to society is $110 billion a year. And teen use of illegal drugs has been on the rise. According to the 1998 National Center on Addiction and Substance Abuse survey, teen marijuana use was up almost 300 percent since 1992. According to the "Monitoring the Future" survey from the University of Michigan, illicit drug use increased for thirteen- and fourteen-year-olds by 51 percent between 1991 and 1999. By 1999, 55 percent of high school seniors reported having used an illicit drug (up from 41 percent just seven years earlier). As parents, we need to take the protection of our children from drug use seriously.

But if we focus our attention only on getting teens to say no to illegal drugs, we'll be missing out on the drug that has by far caused the greatest devastation to their age group—alcohol. According to the Centers for Disease Control and Prevention, the use of alcohol is associated with the leading causes of death and injury among teenagers and young adults (in the form of motor-vehicle crashes, homicides, and suicides). Drunk driving is the cause of over half of all fatal traffic accidents on the weekends, and traffic crashes are the greatest single cause of death for every age from six through thirty-three. Researchers estimate that alcohol use is implicated in one to two thirds of sexual assaults and date-rape cases among teens and college students. People who begin drinking before age fifteen are four times more likely to develop alcoholism than those who begin at age twenty-one. The purchase and possession of alcohol by people under twenty-one is against the law in all fifty states, but our society tacitly condones its use among teens. As of 1996, 37 percent of U.S. male twelfth-graders had participated in binge drinking, and 36 percent were regular drinkers.

We also need to steer our children away from the use of tobacco. More than four hundred thousand people die each year from tobacco-related diseases. Tobacco is responsible for nearly one in every five deaths in the United States. According to the American Cancer Society, of people who have ever smoked daily, 71 percent were smoking daily before age eighteen. Between 1992 and 1997, the percentage of students who reported smoking daily increased from 17 percent to 25 percent. For the long-term benefit of our children's health, we must protect them from the addictive, harmful effects of cigarette smoking.

In all of this, we should keep in mind one last statistic from the Partnership for a Drug-Free America: teens whose parents talk to them regularly about the dangers of drugs are 42 percent less likely to use drugs than those whose parents don't, yet only one in four teens reports having these conversations.

Script on Saying No to Drugs

There are substances that we can take into our bodies that can lead to harm. Some of these things include illegal drugs, alcohol, and tobacco.

We don't ever want you to take illegal drugs. Taking drugs like marijuana, heroin, and cocaine is not only against the law, but over time they can do great damage to people's bodies and minds. Because drugs can be addictive—which means it's very hard to stop taking them once you've started—people can become slaves to them. It can destroy their lives once they start.

We also don't want you to drink alcoholic beverages while you're underage. Drinking alcohol is associated with the leading causes of death and injury among teenagers and young adults. Over half of all fatal traffic accidents on the weekends happen because of drunk driving, and many of those involve young people. Just as you can overdose on drugs, drinking too much can kill you. Some people can become severely addicted to alcohol—an illness we call alcoholism. Alcoholism can be very harmful to a person's body, mind, and happiness. While you're young, we want you to be especially safe and not drink. It's against the law for people younger than age twenty-one to buy and have alcoholic beverages.

And finally, we also don't want you to smoke or to use other tobacco products. More than four hundred thousand people die each year from tobacco-related diseases. People can cut their life span by twenty to twenty-five years if they smoke. And most people who smoke started before they were eighteen. By using it when they're young, kids can become addicted to tobacco, and quitting is very hard.

You need to always feel free to talk to me about these things. Many kids are pressured at some time to use drugs and alcohol. I know what that's like. It's sometimes hard to say no to your friends—but in this case, your life and the lives of others depend on it. I can help you practice different ways to say no.

Questions to Ask Your Kids

■■ Do you understand why it's not a good idea to use drugs, alcohol, and tobacco?

■■ Have you ever felt pressured to use any of these things?

■■ How could you respond to that kind of pressure?

SAYING NO TO TEEN SEX

Note to Parents

Sexual mores have changed significantly in our country over the past generation. The upside of this has been the development of more positive and less inhibited attitudes about sex. The downside has been that our society is even more preoccupied with sex and has minimized the value of sexual responsibility and restraint. This lack of restraint (especially since the 1970s) has contributed significantly to a large increase in broken marriages, broken families, teenage sexual activity, teen pregnancies, teens becoming parents before they're financially and emotionally ready, unwanted and uncared-for children, physical disease, and an increase in abortions.

In the same way that we teach our children to say no to drugs, we must also teach them to say no to teen sex. While the percentage of twelfth-graders in the United States who have had sex decreased from 72 percent to 61 percent between 1990 and 1997, this remains a high number. The United States has by far the highest teen pregnancy rate of any industrialized country. According to the 1996 report *U.S. Teenage Pregnancy Statistics*, four out of ten girls at that time were getting pregnant in the United States before age twenty. These pregnancies often end in births. The young women usually do not have male support, and often lack the emotional and financial resources to fully care for their children (few of these teen mothers give their children up for adoption, and 80 percent of unwed mothers end up on welfare).

In addition to unwanted pregnancy, each year more than three million teens contract a sexually transmitted disease (STD). Young people have been particularly vulnerable to HIV, hepatitis B, and gonorrhea. Sexually active young people can develop sexual habits and attitudes that are destructive to their emotional development and to their future adult and family relationships.

Almost all cultural and religious traditions of the past have maintained that it's better for the emotional, physical, and spiritual lives of unwed teenagers to refrain from sexual activity. As we have seen sexual mores change, the wisdom of this moral rule has been borne out.

According to the 1999 Youth Risk Behavior Survey, 93 percent of high school–age teens said it's important that they be given a strong message from society to abstain from teen sex. The script below is in line with both this desire and with traditional cultural and religious sexual mores. This traditional view is not always emphasized in our secular society. Whatever view you hold, you need to spell it out clearly. If children are left to drift on this subject, they may make choices that bring great unhappiness and that do harm to themselves and others. Their friends and the media, via TV programs and movies, will teach them if you don't. Given the realities of our current society, experts recommend talking to children about sex starting at eight to ten years old. We also need to shield our children from programs, movies, and music that contain adult-level sexual content.

Script to Introduce Saying No to Teen Sex

It's with good reason that major religions and many wise people have always included chastity as part of their moral code. Chastity means not having sex before getting married. Some movies and TV programs show situations where young people have sexual relationships before they get married—so it's very important that we discuss this subject directly and clearly.

One of the most important human relationships is a sexual relationship. It's a very special and close relationship between a man and a woman. A sexual relationship means that you make a strong commitment to another person. It means that you're potentially willing to have and raise children with that person. Teenagers are too young to make this kind of commitment to a single person. Even if teenagers really like someone, they're too young to make long-term commit-

ments that include sex. Sexual relationships are meant for adults who have a strong commitment to each other.

God has shared with us this wonderful power to create life. It's a power that can bring emotional and physical joy to the relationship between a man and a woman. But as with any physical or mental power, it needs to be used with care and wisdom. When it's used carelessly, it can be destructive. Teenage sex can result in physical disease, children coming into the world without adult parents, teens having to be parents way before they're ready to and before they've been able to live a full single life, abortions, and much emotional pain and suffering.

You need to say no to teen sex in the same way that you need to say no to drugs. During your life, you'll come to know young people who have such relationships. Teen sex is not a good choice, but it's important not to condemn these people. Everyone makes his or her own choices. But it's important that you choose to not be involved in sex when you're a teenager. If you ever feel pressured in this area, we should talk about it.

Questions to Ask Your Kids

- Why is it important for teens to say no to teen sex?
- What could you do if you felt pressured by others to have sex?
- To emphasize traditional views about sex before marriage, you can also ask: Why would it be good to wait until marriage to have sex?

AVOIDING HARMFUL MEDIA
AND PEER INFLUENCES

Note to Parents

Each of us is blessed with a unique spiritual life—a life of thoughts, beliefs, imagination, feelings, ideas, intuitions, intentions, willpower, and memories. Just as we can help preserve good physical health, we can preserve good spiritual health. I define good spiritual health as simply: (1) general inner well-being and resilience; and (2) a general desire to refrain from harm and to do good. Good influences enhance this spiritual health, and bad influences diminish it.

Children are born with predispositions when it comes to their inner lives. Some kids are inherently more timid, bold, kind, aggressive, upbeat, or melancholy by nature. But as Daniel Goleman points out in his book *Emotional Intelligence*, "temperament is not destiny." Children learn as they grow, and the beliefs and attitudes they develop over time will greatly influence their inner lives—either amplifying or muting the less positive aspects of their temperaments.

Parents, family, friends, school, church, TV, and movies can all influence our children's internal beliefs, thinking habits, attitudes, and rules for living. As parents, we can be a primary positive influence in their lives, especially when our kids are young, but they can also be influenced by anything they have a lot of contact with. Two of the strongest outside influences for our children are media (entertainment) and peer influences. Destructive media and peer influences can amplify a child's negative beliefs and attitudes, creating unhappiness and greater potential for doing harm.

Elements of the entertainment industry have become to our children's souls what the tobacco companies are to our children's physical health. Some entertainment producers seem to have as little regard for the spiritual and moral well-being of our children as tobacco producers have for physical health. They sometimes seem bent on amplifying ideas and images that might bring our children harm, rather than helping us to mute those messages. Messages of violence, unrestrained sex, and extreme vulgarity and obscenity (particularly from the music industry) have become everyday fare. The entertainment industry's influence is particularly harmful for those children in our society who have a greater natural tendency toward aggressive, risky behavior. We must resolve to shield our children from the worst of the entertainment industry's offerings. We also need to keep them from hanging around peers who can influence them in bad ways.

Script to Introduce Avoiding Harmful Media and Peer Influences

As humans, we're blessed not only with a physical body but also with a life inside of us—a life of thoughts, feelings, willpower, and memories. Just as there are things that can harm our bodies, there are also things that can harm us inside.

Harmful spiritual influences include anything that: (1) makes us feel unhappy or angry inside too often, or (2) makes us want to do bad things to others. Good spiritual influences help us to feel happy inside and keep us from doing harm. Spiritual influences can include family, friends, school, movies, TV, music, or anything else that we have a lot of contact with.

When you're older, you can make your own choices about the movies and TV programs that you watch and the music you listen to. But while you're young, we'll figure out together the rules regarding these things so that we're comfortable with them as your parents. Some movies, TV programs, and music just aren't good for kids (or adults, for that matter).

We don't want you to watch TV programs or movies that have a lot of violence or sex, or to look at websites with those kinds of things. If people watch too much violence, they can lose their reverence for life, and violence can seem not nearly as bad as it really is after a while. And while sex is a wonderful thing, it's a private experience meant for adults—not to be watched on TV by kids. We don't want you to watch R-rated movies. We also don't want you to listen to music that is about violence, sex, hating people, or that has a lot of swearwords.

The friends you choose are important. Friends can have either a good or bad influence on us. If we see that friends of yours are a bad influence, we're going to ask you not to hang out with them. A bad influence would be if they're getting you to do bad things or if they're causing you a lot of unhappiness. We want you to be around people who help you feel good, not people who make you feel bad or get you to do bad things.

Having fun is also part of being happy. We want you to do lots of fun things in life. But you need to find fun things that don't do harm to you or others.

Questions to Ask Your Kids

- Do you understand what spiritual influence means?
- What kinds of movies, TV programs, music, and friends would not be good for us?
- How can people still have fun and avoid bad influences?

Virtues of Treatment of Others

NONHARM

Note to Parents

There is a Hindu principle of living called *ahimsa*, which means to live a life of noninjury to living beings. *Ahimsa* was a guiding principle for Mahatma Gandhi in both his public and private life. If we do nothing else, we make a great contribution to the world by simply trying not to do harm to others. The moral elements of the Ten Commandments are centered around this principle: not killing, not stealing, not lying, not wanting other people's things. The world would truly become a heaven on earth if nonharm became the vow of all people.

Teaching our children the rule of nonharm is the most fundamental social virtue we can teach them. All of us do hurtful things from time to time; this is part of being a human being. But our children need to be taught to avoid major harm (violence, cruelty, stealing) and to learn from any harmful acts and not repeat them. Doing good deeds in the world isn't the only way to make a positive contribution to society (though doing good deeds is a great thing). Our children make a contribution to their community just by avoiding harm.

We also need to teach our kids to change harmful behavior. Doing hurtful things to others from time to time is unavoidable. But it's also in our power to change habitual behavior that hurts others and ourselves. Children should learn to recognize harmful behavior, apologize for it, make up for it, and decide to stop doing it. In theological parlance, they need to learn the principle of repentance.

Script to Introduce Nonharm

One of the most important things to learn in life is not to do harm to other people. Just think what the world would be like if we all decided not to do anything that would be harmful to others. There wouldn't be wars, crime, or many of the other problems we have in the world. The world would be even greater than it is if all people made the choice to try not to harm one another.

All of us do or say hurtful things sometimes; it's part of being human. We might have a hard time, or get in a bad mood, and say or do something that hurts another person's feelings. But it's very important not to do really harmful or dangerous things to other people. The Ten Commandments are special rules for life found in the Bible [the full Ten Commandments are found in Exodus 20:1–17*] and many of those rules are about not doing serious harm to others. Some of these rules are:

1. *Do not kill*
2. *Do not steal things from others*
3. *Do not lie about others*

We have set up rules in our own family about not doing harm to one another. These rules not only make our family life better, they

---

*To paraphrase the Ten Commandments:
1. Worship only God
2. Don't worship things
3. Keep God's name holy
4. Rest and pray on the Sabbath
5. Respect your parents
6. Don't murder
7. Be faithful in your marriage
8. Don't steal
9. Don't lie
10. Don't be greedy or envious

prepare you to not do harm as you get older [this would be a good time to review those rules]. Always try to remember to treat others as you would like to be treated. You don't have to be friends with everyone, or like everyone in the same way, but you need to keep yourself from doing harmful things to others.

When you hurt someone else, we want you to apologize, make up for the hurt as best you can, and learn from the experience so you don't do it again. When you apologize, first say what you did wrong: "I'm sorry I called you that name." Then try to make up for it: "I won't do it again." When you apologize, take responsibility for what you did, no matter what the other person did. And when you say you're sorry, it's important to really mean it. Again, you don't have to be friends with everybody, but we want you to be respectful to everybody.

If you've done harm to someone else's property, do your best to make up for it. If you broke a window with your baseball, we expect you to pay for the new window. If you're not sure how you can make up for the harm you caused, you can always say, "I'm so sorry for what I did. How can I make it up to you?"

Remember, part of being human is making mistakes. We don't want you to beat yourself up about making mistakes, but it's important to learn from them and stop doing them. If we don't learn from harmful mistakes, we can develop harmful habits that bring pain and unhappiness to ourselves and others.

Questions to Ask Your Kids

■ ■ What types of actions can do major harm to others?
■ ■ Can you think of laws we have to keep people from harming one another?
■ ■ Why do you think these laws are important?
■ ■ What would the world be like if we all made a decision not to harm other people?

KINDNESS

Note to Parents

The most fundamental form of kindness is living by the rule of nonharm. But kindness can have many other faces: fairness, sympathy, compassion, mercy, forgiveness, patience, and providing a helping hand. It means not only refraining from harming others but going out of our way to benefit others, without concern for what we receive in return. Acts of kindness recognize that everyone else is another "I." I've heard it said that trying to help other countries in need of serious humanitarian aid is only a "drop in the bucket," since there's so much poverty in the world. But if that drop were our mother, our brother, our daughter, or our son, we would do whatever we could to help. Kindness is humanity and love in action. It's treating others as we would like to be treated on a proactive basis. Loving kindness is the binding, healing power within our human universe. It binds marriages, families, communities, and nations together. Hate and cruelty tear the world apart.

Script to Introduce Kindness

Kindness is treating others as you would want to be treated. It's treating others with kind and helpful words and deeds.

A big part of kindness is simply not harming others. It's kind not to harm others physically or say mean things to them or about them. The world would be a very kind place if we all just did that. But kindness means even more than not harming others. It also means going out of our way to help others. This can involve sharing what we have with others in need, helping others do something when they need a hand, saying a kind word to others when they feel sad, listening to others when they need someone to talk to, or stopping our friends from doing unkind things to other kids.

When we act in kindness, we put aside our own interests and pay attention to others in need. Some people, like Mother Teresa of Calcutta, have dedicated their whole lives to helping others with loving kindness. Mother Teresa spent almost all of her life taking care of people in India who were very sick, very poor, and very lonely. She also helped babies and children who had no parents.

It's good to remember that everyone else is another person just like you or me. They are somebody else's son or daughter, brother or sister. They have feelings and fears, they can feel pain and sadness, and they want to be accepted by other people. They need food, clothing, and safety. They also experience hard times and problems, and they want to be treated with kindness. Kindness is what brings the world together. Unkindness is what tears the world apart.

Questions to Ask Your Kids

- ■■ Have you ever had people do kind things for you? What kinds of things? How did you feel?
- ■■ Have you ever had people do unkind things to you? What kinds of things? How did you feel?
- ■■ Why is it sometimes hard to be kind?
- ■■ Have you ever seen someone at school who is lonely, sad, or needs help? What could you do to be kind in those situations?
- ■■ Why is it important to give to charities to help other people?

HONESTY

Note to Parents

Honesty, like justice, is part of our social contract. Society erupts into chaos if there isn't faith in a strong system of honesty. Hearkening to the concept of natural, moral law (What would the world be like if everyone lived by this rule?), think of a world in which everyone lived by the rule of dishonesty. We couldn't depend on our marriages, families, government, justice system, banks and financial system, schools, or anything else. These institutions and any others would either disintegrate or be maintained only by armed force (which is what often happens in nations corrupted by rampant dishonesty). If institutions can't be counted on to be honest, then people will not trust them or use them. Honesty is the coin of the realm that makes everything else work in a society. Honesty is so important that societies establish numerous laws to uphold truth-telling in the dealings that people have with one another.

As with institutions, so it is with individuals. We lose our credibility and legitimacy if we allow dishonesty to become part of our individual nature. Our spouses, children, coworkers, lenders, and anyone else we deal with will no longer trust us or want to associate with us if we are cankered by dishonesty. Undoubtedly we soon would not even know or trust ourselves. The strength of our relationships is based on a solid foundation of honesty.

Script to Introduce Honesty

What would it be like to live in a world where nobody told the truth? We wouldn't be able to trust our family, friends, neighbors, teachers, police officers, stores, or anybody else. It would be terrible, because we would never be able to believe what others told us or taught us.

Honesty is one of the most important things for a country to have. Honesty creates trust, which means being able to believe what people say. Without trust, people won't want to work, play, or live around one another. They won't believe the store where they buy things, they won't believe teachers they learn from, and they won't believe the police and fire officers who are supposed to protect them. For this reason, countries have laws to protect people from the dishonesty of others.

What is true of countries is also true for individuals. If we tell lies to people, they will start not to believe us—they won't trust us. If they don't trust us, they won't want to work, play, or be with us. We would find our lives becoming very difficult and unhappy. If we get in the habit of telling lies, it will be harder for us to know and tell the truth to ourselves.

It's hard to tell the truth when we think we might get in trouble, but it's the right thing to do and usually things only get worse by lying. In rare situations, it's okay to tell a lie in order to protect ourselves or others from dangerous people. And if our words might hurt other people, it's not necessary to say everything we think or know if it's not an important issue. But as a general rule, it's very important to be honest.

In our family, we need to have a deal: you need to always tell us the truth, and we need to not get overly upset when you tell us the truth about things that we may not like (like admitting to making a mistake or breaking a rule). Remind us of this deal if we forget. We need to be able to trust one another in our family. Telling the truth is the best way to treat other people. It's good for people to be able to trust our word.

Questions to Ask Your Kids

- ■ ■ Why is honesty so important?
- ■ ■ Why do you think people sometimes lie?
- ■ ■ What would it be like to live in a world full of dishonesty?
- ■ ■ Are you ever afraid to tell the truth because you think you'll be punished? What can you do when you're afraid to tell the truth?

COMMUNITY SERVICE

Note to Parents

Community service is showing kindness at the community level. It's doing things that both benefit people and share our uniqueness with the world. In his book *Wherever You Go, There You Are*, Jon Kabat-Zinn tells the story of Buckminster Fuller's contemplated suicide at the age of thirty-two. Fuller, an architect, engineer, philosopher, inventor, and futurist, had experienced a series of business failures that left him feeling he had made such a mess of his life that his wife and young daughter would be better off without him. But then he had a revelation that changed his life. The inspiration came to him to live as though he *had* died. Being dead, he wouldn't have to worry about how things worked out for him personally, and he'd be free to live as a representative of the universe. This new perspective completely transformed his approach to living. The rest of his life would be a gift. His guiding question became "What is it on this planet that needs doing that I know something about, that probably won't happen unless I take responsibility for it?" Kabat-Zinn phrases the question in a different way: "What is my job on the planet with a capital 'J'?" or "What do I care about so much that I would pay to do it?"

Sharing ourselves with our communities is sharing our unique personalities, interests, and skills. In particular, it's sharing our uniqueness in ways that leave the world a better place—in even the smallest ways. It's doing the things that may not get done unless we do them. We all have traits or talents that are unique and valuable, and often we don't recognize their value. Some of us have the more publicly recognized gifts of music, art, scientific knowledge, political know-how, or athleticism. But others have the just-as-valuable gifts of listening, talking, sympathizing, peacemaking, working hard, and seeing important things through. We provide community service whenever we let go of ourselves and give our talents, traits, and ambitions to the world. We are all humbled by those who have been willing to give up even life itself to provide service to their communities and countries.

For strong theists who want to know what God would have them do with their lives, community service is a good place to start. Sharing ourselves with the universe is experiencing the full measure of our creation. And maybe the most important community to begin providing our service to is our own family and neighborhood.

Script to Introduce Community Service

God has given all people in the world to one another to help each other in times of need. When we do service to our community, we are showing kindness to lots of people around us, even people we don't know. Community service is sharing our own unique talents, interests, and personalities with the world.

Doing community service includes:

- *Giving a hand to older people in our neighborhood when we see they need help*
- *Being friendly and helpful to others in our neighborhood*
- *Picking up litter*
- *Visiting people in rest homes*
- *Volunteering at a hospital or hospice*
- *Volunteering at libraries, animal shelters, or schools*
- *Participating in community musical, sports, or artistic events*
- *Participating in school or city government*
- *Helping to raise money for a good cause*

Some people, like those in the armed services, police officers, and firefighters, have been willing to give up even their own lives in service to their communities and countries.

Someday you'll use your skills and interests to make a living. But some of your skills and interests might not give you money, fame, or anything at all—they will be gifts that you give to the world. Providing community service means sharing our skills, interests, and money in order to leave the world a better place.

We believe that doing community service is a gift to others and to yourself. It will help you know yourself better and give you a sense of pride and joy to know that you've shared something of yourself with others.

Questions to Ask Your Kids

- ■■ Why is it good to help others in the community?
- ■■ What types of everyday things can we do to help?
- ■■ What types of service do you think are most needed, in either the local community or in the world?
- ■■ What areas of community service do you think would be most interesting to get involved in?

PART FOUR

Partnering with

Organized Religion

Organized Religion As a Resource

❧

As theists, our primary religious identity should logically be as God's creations or children. This identity should bind us to other people, not separate us. If we overidentify with our formal religious group (whether Catholic, Protestant, Jew, Muslim, Hindu, or other), we risk losing sight of this larger picture. Our association with these religious traditions can be supportive, inspiring, strengthening, and enjoyable, but they are not God, and we are not their children. The founders and teachers of these religious traditions would be the first to confirm that their purpose is to point people to God. We are first and foremost God's children. Even for those who believe that their religious group provides the only true way, that way is presumably to God.

My friend's son once asked the good, simple question: "Why does religion have to be organized?" The simple answer is that it doesn't. As Abraham Lincoln exemplified, we don't need a church, temple, or mosque in order to believe in, or pray to, God. We can do that directly. We don't need to go to formal religious services to know right from wrong. We can see for ourselves what hurts people, and we can directly teach our children right from wrong. But organized religion can be a very positive association of people. It can strengthen and enrich our religious and spiritual lives. For the benefit of our children's religious and moral training, some type of institutional involvement may be worth considering.

Religions have developed over time for generally very good

reasons. They have provided human beings with communal ways of worshiping God and helped them commit themselves to living in harmony with God and God's Creation. A religious institution can be a good resource for worshiping God and teaching our children. It can provide the structure and discipline to help us maintain our commitment to God and to our personal moral beliefs and vows. Communal prayers, songs, and readings focused on God can inspire us, comfort us, and return our hearts back to the sacred. We can develop strong friendships that bring us joy and carry us through the ups and downs of life. Religious institutions can provide the organizational muscle for wholesome activities and community service. They can reinforce good values. They can also be a place for our children to meet friends and future soul mates.

Besides offering a place for worship and fellowship, religious institutions also have good materials that we can use in our home-churching activities, including books, lesson manuals, supplies, hymnals, prayer books, and videos. Many of the major denominations have their own publishing houses that produce materials for teaching children. We need to keep in mind, however, that associations of people are meant to support one another. If we choose to associate with an organized religion and use its resources, we need to help out and be a resource to others in the group. We need to contribute both our time and money.

As mentioned previously, we don't have to agree with all the details of an organized religion for it to have value in our lives. We certainly don't agree with everything that happens in our government, our schools, or our workplaces, yet we continue to associate with them because of the net positive value. If the official views of organized religion differ from my own, I am respectful but direct in pointing out my differences to my children. I say, in essence, "This is an area where my own beliefs are different from organized religion, and this is why." I also usually add something like "You'll develop your own thoughts and beliefs about this issue over time. And your beliefs don't need to be the same as mine, any more than my beliefs are exactly as my parents believed. But I want to let you know how I feel about this and why I feel the way I do."

As detailed earlier, our family participates in organized religion on a limited basis. We have loosely adopted the Amish custom of participating in the gathering church every other week or so. Church is not the focus of our family's religious life, but it is a positive association for our children. By giving our children an association with other people of faith, we provide them with another potentially helpful element for their social and moral support system. Depending on their personalities, this support may become valuable to them in their lives. It is our hope that they'll be able to draw on it in times of need.

Contact List for Major Denominations

The *Yearbook of American and Canadian Churches*, published by Abingdon Press (800-672-1789), provides good information on institutionalized religions and denominations found in North America. Below are some of the major religions and denominations in the United States. To learn about their resources, contact them directly. Not all of these groups are set up to respond to the question "Do you have materials I can use to provide religious education in the home?" Nonetheless, there are a few jewels in the group. Information on membership numbers is taken from the *2000 Encyclopaedia Britannica* Book of the Year.

Buddhism

There are approximately 2.6 million Buddhists in North America and 356 million worldwide.

www.dharmanet.com

Christianity

There are approximately 260 million Christians in North America and 2 billion worldwide.

AFRICAN METHODIST EPISCOPAL CHURCH
    Headquarters: 202-371-8700 (Washington, D.C.)
    www.ame-today.com

AMERICAN BAPTIST CHURCHES U.S.A.
    Headquarters: 610-768-2000 (Valley Forge, PA)
    www.abc-usa.org

ASSEMBLIES OF GOD
 Headquarters: 417-862-2781 (Springfield, MO)
 www.ag.org

CHRISTIAN CHURCH (DISCIPLES OF CHRIST)
 Headquarters: 317-635-3100 (Indianapolis, IN)
 www.disciples.org

CHRISTIAN CHURCHES AND CHURCHES OF CHRIST
 Headquarters: 513-598-6222 (Cincinnati, OH)

CHURCH OF CHRIST, SCIENTIST (CHRISTIAN SCIENCE)
 Headquarters (Mother Church): 617-450-3301 (Boston, MA)
 www.tfccs.com

CHURCH OF GOD
 Headquarters: 423-472-3361 (Cleveland, TN)
 www.churchofgod.cc

CHURCH OF GOD IN CHRIST
 Headquarters: 901-578-3800 (Memphis, TN)
 www.cogic.org

CHURCH OF JESUS CHRIST OF LATTER-DAY SAINTS
(MORMON)
 Headquarters: 801-240-1000 (Salt Lake City, UT)
 www.lds.org

CHURCH OF THE NAZARENE
 Headquarters: 816-333-7000 (Kansas City, MO)
 www.nazarene.org

EPISCOPAL CHURCH
 Headquarters: 212-867-8400 (New York, NY)
 www.ecusa.anglican.org

EVANGELICAL LUTHERAN CHURCH IN AMERICA
 Headquarters: 773-380-2700 (Chicago, IL)
 www.elca.org

GREEK ORTHODOX ARCHDIOCESE OF AMERICA
 Headquarters: 212-570-3500 (New York, NY)
 www.goarch.org

JEHOVAH'S WITNESSES
 Headquarters: 718-560-5600 (Brooklyn, NY)
 www.watchtower.org

THE LUTHERAN CHURCH—MISSOURI SYNOD
  Headquarters: 314-965-9917 (St. Louis, MO)
  www.lcms.org

NATIONAL BAPTIST CONVENTION OF AMERICA
  Headquarters: 214-946-8913 (Dallas, TX)
  www.nbcamerica.org

NATIONAL BAPTIST CONVENTION, USA
  Headquarters: 615-228-6292 (Nashville, TN)
  www.nationalbaptist.org

NATIONAL MISSIONARY BAPTIST CONVENTION OF AMERICA
  Headquarters: 323-582-0090 (Los Angeles, CA)
  www.natl-missionarybaptist.com

ORTHODOX CHURCH IN AMERICA (RUSSIAN ORTHODOX)
  Headquarters: 516-922-0550 (Syosset, NY)
  www.oca.org

PENTECOSTAL ASSEMBLIES OF THE WORLD
  Headquarters: 317-547-9541 (Indianapolis, IN)

PRESBYTERIAN CHURCH (U.S.A.)
  Headquarters: 502-569-5000 (Louisville, KY)
  www.pcusa.org

PROGRESSIVE NATIONAL BAPTIST CONVENTION
  Headquarters: 202-396-0558 (Washington, D.C.)
  www.pnbc.org

THE ROMAN CATHOLIC CHURCH (U.S. CATHOLIC CONFERENCE)
  Headquarters: 202-541-3000 (Washington, D.C.)
  www.nccbuscc.org

THE SALVATION ARMY
  Headquarters: 703-684-5500 (Alexandria, VA)
  www.salvationarmy.org

SEVENTH-DAY ADVENTIST CHURCH
  Headquarters: 301-680-6000 (Silver Spring, MD)
  www.adventist.org

SOCIETY OF FRIENDS (QUAKERS)
  Friends General Conference: 215-561-1700 (Philadelphia, PA)
  www.fgcquaker.org

SOUTHERN BAPTIST CONVENTION
   Headquarters: 615-244-2355 (Nashville, TN)
   www.sbc.net
UNITARIAN UNIVERSALIST ASSOCIATION
   Headquarters: 617-742-2100 (Boston, MA)
   www.uua.org
UNITED CHURCH OF CHRIST
   Headquarters: 216-736-2100 (Cleveland, OH)
   www.ucc.org
THE UNITED METHODIST CHURCH
   Headquarters: 800-251-8140
   www.umc.org
UNITED PENTECOSTAL CHURCH INTERNATIONAL
   Headquarters: 314-837-7300 (Hazelwood, MO)
   www.upci.org
UNITY CHURCH
   Headquarters: 816-524-7414 (Lee's Summit, MO)
   www.unity.org

Hinduism

There are approximately 1.3 million Hindus in North America and 800 million worldwide.
   www.hindu.org

Islam

There are approximately 4.4 million Muslims in North America and 1.2 billion worldwide.
   www.islam.org
   www.ias.org (Sufism)

Judaism

There are approximately 6 million Jews in North America and 14 million worldwide.

RABBINICAL COUNCIL OF AMERICA (ORTHODOX)
   Headquarters: 212-807-7888 (New York, NY)
   www.rabbis.org

UNION OF AMERICAN HEBREW CONGREGATIONS (REFORM)
    Headquarters: 212-650-4000 (New York, NY)
    http//uahc.org

THE UNITED SYNAGOGUE OF CONSERVATIVE JUDAISM
    Headquarters: 212-533-7800 (New York, NY)
    www.uscj.org

Bahá'i

There are approximately 770,000 Bahá'is in North America and 7 million worldwide.
    www.us.bahai.org

Jainism

There are approximately 7,000 Jains in North America and 4 million worldwide.
    www.jainworld.com

Shintoism

There are approximately 56,000 Shintoists in North America and 3 million worldwide.
    www.shinto.org

Sikhism

There are approximately 500,000 Sikhs in North America and 23 million worldwide.
    www.sikhs.org

A BRIEF HISTORY
OF FAMILY RELIGIOUS LIFE

DURING THE YEAR'S TIME I SPENT TIME RESEARCHING THE history of family-based religion, I was fascinated to discover that religion originated with the family. The first altar of religion was found not in a church but around the family hearth. The first priests and priestesses were fathers and mothers. Indeed, the vast majority of our "revealed" religions were revealed not by professional priests but by everyday—though extraordinary—family members (Abraham, Jesus, Mohammed, Siddhartha). As long as there have been human family groups on the earth, we have had a deep-seated interest in spiritual and religious matters. Some of the beliefs inspired by these interests were passed on from one generation to the next, and as family groups merged into tribes, some of their beliefs also merged. As tribes merged into states, the state religions also assimilated elements of family and tribal beliefs.

In the traditional world, the family was the center of social and economic life. The family was the setting for almost all social functions—including welfare, education, religion, and recreation. In the modern Western world, we can't appreciate the all-encompassing, central role that the family group played in the religious lives of individuals. Grandfathers, not priests, presided over religious worship and rites. Even with the rise of an institutional priesthood and temples outside of the family, the household was held sacred and remained the primary seat of faith and worship. Just as the modern "State" has taken over much from the family by way of the protection, education, and welfare of individuals, so the modern "Church" has assumed much of the religious function of families.

Family structures in the ancient world weren't ideal. The patriarchal, patrilineal family patterns of the past were frequently controlling and autocratic. The father's authority was often absolute, with women, children, and younger men of households marginalized. In many cultures, people found their primary identity in their family rather than in themselves. People outside of household systems, particularly in Rome and China, were dealt with as nonpersons.

Nonetheless, the family took primary responsibility for the material and spiritual well-being of its members in ways that are telling for us today. If families could be smothering, they could also be highly supportive. People had a clear identity and a strong social support system to help them through the ups and downs of life.

There's a remarkably consistent pattern in cultures of the past relating to family religion. Family religion—the religion of the household—has been at the very core of cultural and societal traditions of the past. Below are some brief summaries that provide a glimpse of what family religious life was like in some of these cultures.

Certainly some religious traditions of the past were harmful, burdensome, and even dangerous. But others sought to simply help adherents worship God in the best ways they knew how. As we consider religions of the past, and find ourselves passing judgment on the "primitiveness" of their faith, we might consider the words of Maximus of Tyre (from *The Enlightened Mind*, edited by Stephen Mitchell), who lived from 125 to 185 A.D.

God himself, the father and fashioner of all that is, older than the sun or sky, greater than time and eternity and all the flow of being, is unnamable by any lawgiver, unutterable by any voice, not to be seen by any eye. But we, being unable to apprehend his essence, use the help of sounds and names and pictures, of beaten gold and ivory and silver, of plants and rivers, mountain peaks and torrents, yearning for the knowledge of him, and in our weakness naming all that is beautiful in this world after his nature—just as happens to earthly lovers. To them the most beautiful sight will be the actual lineaments of the beloved. But for remembrance' sake they will be happy in the sight of a lyre, a little spear, a chair perhaps, or a running ground, or anything in the world that awakens the memory of the beloved. Why should I further examine and pass judgment about images? Let men know what is divine. Let them know. That is all. If a Greek is stirred to the remembrance of God by the art of Phidias, . . . another by a river, another by fire, I have no anger for their divergences. Only let them know, let them love, let them remember.

■ African Family Religion ■

Though we do not have many written historical records of Africa, we know through archaeology that the ancient tribes and nations enjoyed rich family and religious traditions. Ancient hunters of the Sahara began, from 8000 B.C. onward, to shape ritual rock paintings as forms of religious art. Typical religious traditions in Africa maintained belief in a supreme high god (who created the world) while also revering lesser sacred forces and local minor gods.

All of African society revolved around well-marked social structures of extended family and clan groups organized into tribes (and in some cases into nation-states). Common to all of these structures was a strong sense of community. As with later Chinese and Roman cultures, the identity of individuals was found in their family and clan membership.

Of primary importance to most African forms of worship was

the family religion. As with other historical cultures, African tribal-based culture placed great emphasis on veneration of family and ancestors. Communion and harmony between one's living family, tribe, and ancestors were key to daily rituals.

Additionally, the African religions placed humans in emphatic communion with the natural world. Religion and spirituality pervaded everyday life, as people recognized and revered the divine in everything around them. Unlike many modern societies, African society made little distinction between the temporal and spiritual worlds. Religious thought and practice wasn't a sabbath ritual but the essence of everyday life. For this reason, African society offered a cordial reception to other religions when they were introduced (Islam, Christianity, and Judaism)—and adopted them into everyday spirituality.

To the present day, religion and spirituality play a central role in African family life. Families participate both domestically and communally in traditional religious rituals, music, and festivities.

■ Hebrew Traditions ■

Throughout Mesopotamia, the family religion was the most fundamental vehicle for religion. Private religion was dedicated to the gods of one's own family (the "gods of the fathers"). Worship of these gods and remembrance of ancestors were instrumental to properly serve and respect one's clan. When Abraham (the father of the Hebrew nation) left Mesopotamia, he took his extended family. Abraham was not formally a priest or prophet; he was a patriarch—the father of his household. He initially officiated over private family worship.

The Hebrews were originally a nomadic desert people with a pastoral economy. As in Africa, beyond the immediate family, one identified with one's clan (a group of related kinsmen). Several clans made up a tribe, and twelve tribes eventually constituted the nation of Israel. During the nomadic period, religion was primarily a private matter. The patriarch served as priest at worship and presided over ceremonial activities.

In the sixth century B.C., Israel was conquered by the Babylonians and came under the control of the Romans. Public authorities expanded control over the Israelite society, including marriage and family. The power of the religious functionaries—the rabbis—emerged during this period, but rabbis did not at first challenge the power of the patriarchs. Rabbinical law and authority eventually became the foundation for marriage and family life.

Despite this transition, the Jewish religious tradition remained deeply woven in the fabric of Jewish family life. In the Greco-Roman world, there had never been a parallel to the devotion of one whole day in seven (the Sabbath) to religion and family. Family celebration of festivals and observance of Sabbath laws continued to closely match the practice of Jews in the public domain.

Today, the home of devoted Jews remains the first altar of family religious life. The altar of the temple was in essence replaced by the family's meal table, and certain family meals became, in part, religious ritual. The Jewish Sabbath is spent primarily at home. Jewish festivals remain both communal and domestic. Many traditions are centered around family religious rituals. Fathers and mothers continue to pronounce holy blessings upon their children.

■ Chinese Worship ■

Under ancient tradition, the extended Chinese family would live together for nine generations before a division of property occurred. The *tsu*, or clan, was composed of all people of a given surname descending from a common ancestor. The *tsu* served as a buffer between the extended family and the larger society and performed educational, welfare, religious, and judicial functions.

Huston Smith, one of the world's preeminent authorities on world religions, has stated that the religion of China has historically been the family. Four thousand years ago, ancestral religion was central to Chinese culture, and the royal ancestral temple was the center of political administration for a clan's village. As with African society, religion pervaded the everyday life of Chinese families. Chinese homes were filled with relics, shrines, incense, and candles dedicated to the remembrance and honor of deceased relatives and to deity. Religious rites were performed at the family level, often with the oldest son serving as the family priest. Eventually, Confucian ideals came to dominate Chinese life for over two thousand years. In turn, these ideals were centered fundamentally around proper relationships within families and within society at large. The family was the center of the Confucian ethic and philosophy. Even as various religious systems developed or were imported into China (Taoism and Buddhism), Confucianism and family relationships remained at their center. Since Taoism and Buddhism were religions oriented toward personal spirituality, they were easily adopted into the Chinese culture of family. This same emphasis on family-based religion and culture also developed in Korea and Japan.

■ Greek and Roman Traditions ■

The original Indo-European tribes of the steppe land of Central Asia migrated north, east, and west. Those who migrated north became the Scandinavians; those who went east became the Persians, Armenians, and Aryans; and those who migrated west became the Greeks, Romans, and pre-European tribes.

The family religious patterns of these early Indo-Europeans were particularly strong. In Roman culture, the family was part of a larger group called the *gens*. The *gens* was composed of all families that traced descent from a common male ancestor. In earliest Roman times, the *gens* held property, conducted religious services, maintained burial grounds, and passed rules that were binding on all members of the *gens*. In ancient Rome, there was no place for a person unaffiliated with a *gens*. Everyone belonged to a household and came under the control of the family head, and the household came under the strong influence of the *gens*.

In the classic work *The Ancient City* (written by Fustel de Coulanges in 1864), we learn that the religious life of early Greeks and Romans centered on the domestic religion, the spiritualization of family life. Each family group had its own ceremonies, its own prayers, and its own hymns. Families gathered around the family hearth in the morning, afternoon, and evening for religious hymns and prayers. Every household had its sacred flame that was kept burning by the vigilant devotion of the women of the home. The flame was kept in remembrance of the family's ancestors. The father was the priest of the home and performed the religious ceremonies. Eventually, there was a pontiff who oversaw religious issues throughout the Roman Empire. However, the pontiff's role was to ensure that fathers continued the religious traditions of their family groups, not to provide content for those traditions.

The mythological religions of Greece and Rome we're familiar with had little bearing on the actual daily religious life of the people. The Olympian gods were more literary figures than they were objects of worship. The domestic religion was the living religion of everyday life.

■ Hindu Traditions ■

As mentioned above, when the Indo-European tribes of Central Asia migrated, the eastward migrants who entered northern India (between 1750 and 1200 B.C.) were known as Aryans. These tribes brought with them religious traditions found in other Indo-European cultures (some scholars have found similarities between early Hindu gods and Greek and Roman gods). These traditions were a major influence, along with native religions, in the early development of Hinduism. The ritual verses and hymns (Vedas) of the Aryans formed the basis for the first Hindu scripture. Additionally, these Indo-Europeans also brought with them the ritual of the sacred family flame. Interest in the religious symbolism of fire (and water) has continued in the Hindu culture to the present day.

The word "Hindu" literally means the religion of India. Initially, there was a very strong priest class. The Brahmins were Aryan priests who offered sacrifices to the various Aryan gods. Over time, the religious practices of India evolved into household rituals, even though there would be thousands of formal religious temples scattered throughout India. Today, as in times past, most Hindu worship *(puja)* takes place in the home. In both rural and urban Hindu homes, a worship area displays the images of favorite deities, and many families observe a morning ritual of prayers, songs, washings, and sacrifices. Congregational worship is rare. Many Hindu idols and shrines are maintained and revered throughout society as symbols of the divine.

In addition to household-based religion, Hinduism has developed several paths to God to reflect the strengths, interests, and personalities of different adherents. The four major paths include knowledge (Jnana Yoga), love (Bakhti Yoga), work (Karma Yoga), and meditation (Raja Yoga). Religion pervades everyday family life in India in ways that are significantly different from the compartmentalized, secular ways of modern Western culture.

■ Early Christian Roots ■

Jesus of Nazareth was a Jew, and he studied Jewish scripture. He was also the leader and teacher of a new religious movement. As with other Jewish teachers and prophets, he emphasized the supreme rule of God. In a world dominated by military and commercial kingdoms, Jesus sent out his disciples to challenge people to be part of the kingdom of God—a kingdom not of castles and soldiers, but of the spirit, open to all people (including the poor and disenfranchised) who chose to live under God's rule. Jesus' program appears to have been primarily a "house" mission, dedicated to visiting the peasant households of Israel.

Early Christians met together in household gatherings—either as a family group or with other Christians in the immediate vicinity. Such gatherings typically did not exceed thirty people. Gatherings included readings, hymns, and a common meal. Not until the third century is there evidence that special buildings were constructed for Christian gatherings. And even in those cases, they were modeled after the rooms into which guests were received in the typical Greek or Roman household. It's reasonable to believe that Christians maintained the strong family structures reflecting their heritage—Jewish or Roman.

Early Christian beliefs had a great deal to do with the family. Christians spoke out strongly against the ways of Rome: adultery, divorce, abortion, and infanticide were aggressively condemned. Many of the earliest Christian fathers held lofty views of marriage, for Jesus approved of it. Over time, these views of marriage changed, until by 402 A.D., priests in the church were required to remain single. For a period of time, the Christian Church was primarily interested in the family as a vehicle for the indoctrination of children. Gradually, more sanguine, supportive views of the family reemerged.

▓ Europe in the Middle Ages ▓

The kinship system of the Germanic and English people of the Middle Ages was quite different from the purely patrilineal structures of the ancient Hebrews, Greeks, and Romans. Both peoples practiced a double descent structure based on the father's and mother's lines. These double-descent kin groups were called the *maegth* in Britain and the *sippe* on the Continent. The *sippe* provided for a buffer between the individual and the state, much like the *tsu* in traditional China. A husband's power over his wife was limited by the fact that she remained a member of her own *sippe*.

For centuries, marriage remained a private matter. The ceremony was simple, conducted by the bride's father; no religious officials were involved. The bride's father simply transferred power over her to the husband. Military power, resulting in feudalism, and the growth of ecclesiastical and civil power came to diminish the influence of the *maegth* and *sippe*.

During the Middle Ages and beyond, religion loomed large in people's lives and pervaded thinking about every event and institution. During the Reformation, for both Catholics and Protestants, great emphasis was placed on the father's role as a religious leader and on daily prayer in the household. Scriptures were read nightly, both as a means of maintaining religious devotion in the home and of teaching children to read. For Protestants, the household played the role of Protestant monastery.

Veneration of the family was also a strong feature of worship during this period. There was a proliferation of family chapels as funerary monuments. Every noble castle and palace held family shrines and halls of family portraits. Christians prayed for their ancestors, and some masses were established specifically to honor all the ancestors of a particular household.

▩ Early European-American Religion ▩

Immigrants generally came to America not as extended families but singly and as nuclear families. The conditions of immigration precluded the development of clan structures. The nuclear family and others living within the household replaced the extended family as the core social unit. The frontier further severed ties from kin and increased the isolation of the nuclear family. Children on the frontier rarely knew the direct authority of their grandfathers and consequently never expected to control their own future grandchildren or extended family. Several studies report that colonial nuclear families averaged about six people in size at any one time (although an average of eight or nine children were born to families, infant mortality was high).

The colonial family performed almost every social and economic service for its members. It was not just an educational unit but a religious one as well. In the north, the orientation was Puritan (Congregationalist), and in the south it was Anglican, but in both cases the family was a religious unit organized around the father, who directed reading of the scriptures, family prayers, and hymn singing. While churchgoing was considered desirable (and even mandatory in the north for a time), it was secondary to the importance of the performance of family religious duties. On the eve of the American Revolution, just 17 percent of the colonial population affiliated with a formal religious body (see *The Churching of America 1776–1990*, by Roger Finke and Rodney Stark).

▓ Modern American Family Religious Life ▓

Since the end of World War II, the influence and power of the family in the United States has subsided. However, religion continues to play an active role in family life. In particular, ethnic groups within the Catholic Church (notably Italian, Irish, and Latin-American) keep strong family religious cultures. Protestant African-Americans maintain strong family religious traditions (in a 1999 Gallup poll, 86 percent of African-Americans, as opposed to 55 percent of Caucasian-Americans, said that religion was "very important" in their lives). Jews and Hindus maintain domestic religious rituals and traditions within the home. Mormons and conservative Christian denominations are also known for fostering family religious life.

Modern family religious life has changed in the United States because families and family life have changed. The following table gives a sense of the changes since 1970:

	1970	1996
Families as a percent of American households	82%	70%
Families with children as a percent of total American families	56%	49%
Families with children as a percent of total American households	46%	34%
Percent of American families headed by a single parent	13%	24%
Percent of two-parent families with children as a percent of total American households	40%	26%
Average family size by number of people	3.58	3.20

Source: *U.S. Bureau of Census data*

Proportionately, there are simply fewer families, fewer families with children, and fewer families with children headed by two parents; and families are smaller. Additionally, it's been estimated that parents have approximately twelve to fourteen fewer hours each week to spend with their children. The confluence of these factors, along with the expanded influence of government and other institutions in the lives of individuals, has reduced the role of family in society. The importance of the role, however, has never been greater. People still enter society through the family, and the impact of family on a person's life remains critical. In a complex world filled with a multitude of options and influences, children more than ever need the kind of sustained guidance and mentoring that only a fully committed and engaged parent can provide.

Americans still consider religion an important part of their lives. In a 1998 Gallup poll, 60 percent of respondents considered religion "very important" in their lives, and 27 percent considered it "fairly important." Forty percent of Americans attend church regularly, which is a much higher rate of participation than in most industrialized nations. In 1998, 67 percent of teens indicated that they felt the need to experience spiritual growth in their lives, compared to 58 percent in 1994 (Emerging *Trends*, June

1999). But people don't necessarily see participation in organized religion as the only way to approach matters of the spirit. According to Gallup data, eight in ten Americans have consistently maintained over the last half-century that one does not need to attend church or synagogue to be a good Christian or Jew. People have become less anchored to specific denominations. An excellent resource for understanding the landscape of religious attitudes of people in the United States is George Gallup's book *Surveying the Religious Landscape: Trends in U.S. Beliefs* (Morehouse Publishing, 1999).

In their book *Shopping for Faith* (Jossey-Bass Publishers, San Francisco, 1998), Richard Cimino and Don Lattin predict that in the new millennium: (1) there will be a growing gap between personal spirituality and religious institutions; and (2) people separated from a religious heritage will seek out new expressions of faith. In this more fluid setting of religious experience, it has become even more important for parents to provide direct religious and moral training for their children. As evidenced by some of the examples in this chapter, there is nothing more "traditional" than the household religion. Home churching is a natural means to help provide our children with a religious and moral foundation.

Sources

Banks, Robert. *Paul's Idea of Community*. Peabody, MA: Hendrickson Publishers, 1994.

Booth, Newell S., Jr., ed. *African Religions: A Symposium*. New York: NOK Publishers, 1977.

Ching, Julia. *Chinese Religions*. New York: Maryknoll, 1993.

Crossan, John Dominic. *The Historical Jesus*. New York: HarperCollins, 1992.

Fustel de Coulanges, Numa Denis. *The Ancient City*. Garden City, NY: Doubleday, 1956 (originally published in 1864).

Gies, Frances and Joseph. *Marriage and Family in the Middle Ages*. New York: Harper and Row, 1987.

Gottlieb, Beatrice. *The Family in the Western World*. Oxford: Oxford University Press, 1993.

Hopfe, Lewis M. *Religions of the World*. Beverly Hills, CA: Glencoe Press, 1976.

Ludwig, Theodore M. *The Sacred Paths of the East*. New York: Macmillan, 1993.

Moxnes, Halvor, ed. *Constructing Early Christian Families*. New York: Routledge, 1997.

Rausch, David A. and Carl Hermann Voss. *World Religions: Our Quest for Meaning*. Minneapolis, MN: Fortress Press, 1989.

Sillery, Anthony. *Africa: A Social Geography*. 2nd ed. New York: Halsted Press, 1972.

Smart, Ninian. *The Religious Experience of Mankind*. New York: Charles Scribner's Sons, 1976.

Ven Der Toom, Karel. *Family Religion in Babylonia, Syria and Israel*. New York: E. J. Brill, 1996.

Yang, C. K. *Religion in Chinese Society*. Berkeley: University of California Press, 1967.

Pulling Together Resources

Some forms of religious and moral training require preparation. Once you figure out what things you want to teach, and how formally or informally you want to teach them, you may need to gather some resources. If you decide that you want to have a family devotional time, a home-based Sunday school, or to use readings, music, or videos in your home-churching process, you'll need to pull together a curriculum or develop a small home-churching library to support those efforts. Fortunately, we live in a time when there are many resources to help us in teaching our children our religious and moral values. But it does take time to sort through and find materials that are congruent with both our personalities and the teachings of our domestic church. If you are committed to the teachings and doctrines of a specific religion and denomination, the search is easier because you can collect some of the materials from the denomination directly (contact information for major denominations in the United States is listed in Part Four). If your beliefs are more independent, you will need to take more time to contact some of the publishers listed below and sift through their catalogs to identify helpful materials. This is something that Julie and I have done ourselves.

The publishers I've listed in this section are some of the ones with which I've become familiar. I've tried to include mostly publishers that have materials for more general audiences, not just their own specific denominations. I've chosen not to list any publishers who may have good resources for children but have chosen to publish disparaging or belittling books about religious traditions that are different from their own. Respectful comparative religious materials are one thing, but materials that ridicule the faith of other cultures and people are at odds with the spirit of love and kinship that should exist among people of faith.

Keep in mind that, in addition to the materials listed below, the newspapers, magazines, and books that we read every day can also be great resources for teaching. As you read good newspaper or magazine articles, clip them out and share them with your children informally or during a family devotional. Many of the classic books of the past also have object lessons in them that are very valuable. There are heroes and good examples all around us if we have eyes that see.

Publishers That Provide Home-Churching Resources

Augsburg Fortress, 800-328-4648, www.augsburgfortress.org

Their "Education Resources" catalog provides numerous resources for teaching religious (Christian-based) and moral beliefs in the home.

Behrman House, 800-221-2755, www.behrmanhouse.com

This publisher provides extensive resources for Jewish family education.

Cokesbury, 800-672-1789, www.cokesbury.org

This publishing arm of the United Methodist Church has an annual catalog that contains Christian-based books, lesson materials, music, and a series for home churching called "Faith Home." They also have a "Children's Resources" catalog.

Children's Ministry, 800-447-1070, www.childrensministry.com

The ministry produces a bimonthly magazine filled with Christian-based teaching resources for children. An annual sourcebook is included in the subscription.

Curriculum Publishing, 800-524-2612

This publishing arm of the Presbyterian Church focuses on religious and moral education. Its "Celebrate Youth" series provides several topical courses for all age groups.

**Dharma Publishing, 800-873-4276,
http://store.dharmapublishing.com**

Dharma publishes Buddhist-based materials for children, including the Jataka Series for Children.

Group Publishing, 800-447-1070, www.grouppublishing.com

Their "Resource" catalog is filled with books, lesson materials, and activity workbooks for Christians of all age groups. Group specializes in providing teaching materials for children and youth.

Hi-Time Pflaum, 800-543-4838, www.hitimepflaum.com

This Catholic-based publisher specializes in religious and moral education. They provide weekly lesson materials for every age group, as well as special books for teaching about sex, drugs, and other areas of parental concern.

IQRA Book Center, 800-521-4272, www.iqra.org

This center provides extensive Islamic education resources for children.

Jewish Lights Publishing, 800-962-4544, www.jewishlights.com

A publisher of the Jewish wisdom tradition for people of all faiths, it provides children's storybooks and other resources to assist in home churching.

Jewish Publication Society, 800-355-1165, www.jewishpub.org

This Jewish-based publisher provides storybooks and other materials for religious and moral education.

Pauline Books & Media, 800-876-4463, www.pauline.org

This Catholic-based publisher provides a variety of storybooks and other materials for teaching children.

St. Mary's Press, 800-533-8095, www.smp.org

This Catholic-based publisher has a particularly large selection of materials for "youth ministry."

Vedic Resource, 800-829-2579, www.vedicresource.com

Vedic provides Hindu-based storybooks for children (look under the "children's" category).

Books That List Resources

Books That Build Character, edited by William Kilpatrick and Gregory and Suzanne M. Wolfe (New York: Simon & Schuster, 1994). This book provides descriptions of more than three hundred classic and popular books that explore moral ground and reinforce qualities of good character.

Children's Books About Religion, by Patricia Pearl Dole (Englewood, CO: Libraries Unlimited, 1999). This is an excellent resource for finding children's books and storybooks relating to general religious themes and for finding children's books regarding specific world religions.

Curriculum of Love, by Morgan Simone Daleo (Charlottesville, VA: Grace Publishing, 1997). This nondenominational book provides extensive exercises and book lists that can be used to enhance children's spiritual development.

Food for the Family Spirit: A Sourcebook for Religious Education, by Laurie N. Bowen (Kansas City, MO: Sheed & Ward, 1997). This book provides a comprehensive list of resources for home religious education for Catholic-oriented parents.

What Stories Does My Son Need?, by Michael Gurian (New York: Putnam, 2000). This book provides a good guide to books and movies that can help to build character in boys (and girls). Not all the recommendations may be appropriate for your home, but this is a good list to start with.

Devotional Books

10-Minute Devotions for Youth Groups, by J. B. Collingsworth (Loveland, CO: Group Publishing, 1989). A series of books that provides devotional ideas with a Christian orientation for teens (also usable for preteens).

Home Altar: Devotions for Families with Children, 800-426-0115, www.augsburgfortress.org. A Christian-based quarterly magazine that provides weekly devotionals that parents can use with their elementary school–age children.

Hot Illustrations for Youth Talks, by Wayne Rice (Grand Rapids, MI: Zondervan Publishing House, 1993). A series of very good stories and illustrations.

How the Children Became Stars, by Aaron Zerah (Notre Dame, IN: Sorin Books, 2000). A very readable, multifaith devotional book organized to provide weekly stories and prayers from around the world. This has become one of my personal favorites.

Journey of Faith Reader and *Journey of Hope Reader*, by Clifford Stevens, (Boys Town, NE: Boys Town Press, 2001). These books feature fables, poems, and real-life stories of inspirational people throughout history. These have recently become some of our favorite resources.

The Ladder, by Edward Hays (Leavenworth, KS: Forest of Peace Publishing, 1999). A book of contemporary parable-stories that will bring some fun and wisdom into family discussions. Edward Hays is a particularly gifted and inspired writer of prayers and devotionals.

The Old Hermit's Almanac: Daily Meditations for the Journey of Life, by Edward Hays (Leavenworth, KS: Forest of Peace Publishing, 1997). A great volume of meditations in the form of an almanac. Contains an interesting historical fact for each day of the year and then spins the fact into a helpful spiritual or moral theme. This is one of our family's favorite resources for readings for our family devotional time.

On This Day, by Robert J. Morgan (Nashville, TN: Thomas Nelson, Publisher, 1997). This Christian-based resource provides an engaging true story for each day of the week taken from the lives of Christian saints, martyrs, and heroes.

The New Century Hymnal (Cleveland, OH: The Pilgrim Press, 1995). This is an excellent compendium of Christian-oriented hymns through time.

The Soul's Almanac, by Aaron Zerah (New York: Penguin Putnam, 1998). An interfaith devotional book with positive thoughts for every day of the year.

Today's Gift: Daily Meditations for Families (Center City, MN: Hazelden Foundation, 1991). Quotes from famous figures through time and from various backgrounds are accompanied with thoughtful reflections for every day of the week. This compact book is another very good source for family devotional readings and discussions.

Treasury of Spiritual Wisdom, by Andy Zubko (San Diego, CA: Blue Dove Press, 1996). A great collection of ten thousand quotations spanning many cultural and religious traditions from East and West.

Worldwide Worship: Prayers, Songs and Poetry, edited by John Marks Templeton Radnor, PA: Templeton Foundation Press, 2000). This is an excellent compilation of religious prayers, songs, and poetry from around the world and from a variety of faith traditions.

Magazines

Devo 'Zine, 800-426-0115, Devo[tional] [Maga]'Zine is a very good Christian-based devotional magazine for teens, published bimonthly by the Upper Room (United Methodist Church). Includes meditations, feature articles, scripture, and other helpful elements.

Guideposts for Kids, 800-932-2145. A value-centered magazine for kids ages seven to twelve. Faith-based with an orientation toward the Christian faith.

Guideposts for Teens, 800-932-2145. Similar to *Guideposts for Kids*, but oriented toward teenagers.

My Friend, 617-541-9805. A Catholic-based magazine for children ages seven to eleven.

Pockets, 800-925-6847. An ecumenical Christian magazine for children ages six to twelve, published by the Upper Room (United Methodist Church). Provides creative activities and stories.

Prayer Books

The Complete Book of Christian Prayer (New York: Continuum Publishing, 2000. A thoughtful compendium of prayers through the ages.

The One World Book of Prayer, edited by Juliet Mabey. (Oxford: OneWorld Publications, 1999). A very good compendium of uplifting and comforting prayers from around the world and from a variety of spiritual and religious traditions.

The Oxford Book of Prayer, edited by George Appleton (New York: Oxford University Press, 1986). A compendium of prayers from various traditions (mostly Christian) and for a variety of occasions.

Prayers for the Domestic Church: A Handbook for Worship in the Home, by Edward Hays (Easton, KS: Forest of Peace Books, 1979). A prayer book especially for home churching. Has additional information helpful for conducting family devotionals and offering parent blessings (800-659-3227). We frequently read prayers from this book during our family devotionals.

Prayers, Praises and Thanksgivings, by Sandol Stoddard (New York: Dial Books, 1997). Upbeat, celebrating, comforting prayers and praises.

Prayers for a Planetary Pilgrim, by Edward Hays (Easton, KS: Forest of Peace Books, 1979). Another one of Edward Hays's very helpful resources. We often read prayers from this book during our family devotionals.

Psalms for Praying, by Nan C. Merrill (New York: Continuum Press, 1998). A reworked version of the Book of Psalms that provides for fresh, contemplative psalms without losing the original essence of this ancient book of prayers.

Books About Prayer

Centering Prayer in Daily Life and Ministry, edited by Gustave Reininger (New York: Continuum Publishing, 1998). This book provides helpful essays in understanding the value and process of contemplative and centering prayer.

Everything Starts from Prayer: Mother Teresa's Meditations on Spiritual Life for People of All Faiths, edited by Anthony Stern (Ashley, OR: White Cloud Press, 1998). An inspiring book that provides the thinking and wisdom of Mother Teresa on the subject of prayer.

Open Mind, Open Heart, by Thomas Keating (New York: Amity House, 1986). A fundamental resource for understanding centering prayer.

The Power of Prayer, edited by Dale Salwak (Novato, CA: New World Library, 1998). An excellent multifaith anthology of thoughts on prayer.

Sacred Texts

There are many editions and translations of traditional sacred texts. Below are some of the most notable ones:

Buddhist

Conze, Edward., trans. *Buddhist Scriptures*. London: Penguin, 1959.

Christian

The Holy Bible: New Revised Standard Version. Oxford: Oxford University Press, 1990.

Hindu

Debroy, Dipavaldi. *The Holy Vedas*, trans. Bibek Debroy. New Delhi, India: BR Publishing, 1999.

Mascaro, Juan, ed., trans. *The Upanishads*. London: Penguin, 1965.

Swami Prabhavananda. *Bhagavad Gita*, trans. Christopher Isherwood. New York: New American Library, 1944; reprint 1995.

Jewish

The Tanakh: The New JPS Translation According to the Traditional Hebrew Text. Philadelphia: Jewish Publication Society, 1988.

Harlow, Rabbi Jules, ed., trans. *The Talmud: Steinsaltz Edition*. New York: Random House, 1990.

Islam

Daewood, N. J., trans. *The Koran*. London and New York: Penguin, 1956; reprint 1990.

Stoic (Greek philosophy school with a strong spiritual and ethical orientation)

Gill, Christopher, ed. *The Discources of Epictetus*. London: J. M. Dent, 1995.

Long, George, trans. *Meditations of Marcus Aurelius*. Amherst, NY: Prometheus, 1991.

Taoist

Mitchell, Stephen, trans. *Tao Te Ching*. San Francisco: Harper & Row, 1988.

Compendia

Ballou, Robert O., ed. *The Portable World Bible*. New York: Penguin, 1976.

Brown, Lewis. *The World's Great Scriptures*. New York: Macmillan, 1973.

Novak, Philip. *The World's Wisdom: Sacred Texts of the World's Religions*. New York: HarperCollins, 1994. This is my personal favorite.

Wilson, Andrew, ed. *World Scripture: A Comparative Anthology of Sacred Texts*. St. Paul, MN: Paragon House, 1995.

Books on Sharing Faith and Values with Children

20 Teachable Virtues, by Barbara C. Unell and Jerry L. Wyckoff (New York: Berkley Publishing Group, 1995). An excellent resource that provides easy-to-use examples of how to teach important virtues to our children through the course of our everyday lives.

Celebrating at Home: Prayers and Liturgies for Families, by Deborah Alberswerth Payden and Laura Loving (Cleveland, OH: United Church Press, 1998). A very good Christian-based resource for prayers and religious celebration traditions in the home.

Everyday Blessings, by Myla and Jon Kabat-Zinn (New York: Hyperion, 1997). An excellent resource to show parents how to enrich their own spiritual lives and the lives of their children through mindful parenting.

Family the Forming Center, by Marjorie Thompson (Nashville, TN: Upper Room Books, 1996). This book, by a Presbyterian minister, reinforces the argument that the domestic church should be at least as integral to our children's spiritual training as the gathering church.

How to Help Your Child Have a Spiritual Life, by Annette Hollander (New York: A&W Publishers, 1980). This book is unfortunately out of print but is available through libraries. Quite a good review of approaches and options available to help children develop spiritually.

Raising Faith-Filled Kids, by Tom McGrath (Chicago: Loyola Press, 2000). While this book is directed in particular to Catholic parents, it's a good resource for all parents on building religion and spirituality into daily family life.

Other Helpful Books

A World of Faith, by Peggy Fletcher Stack and Kathleen Peterson (Salt Lake City: Signature Books, 1998). A simple, respectful book that briefly reviews the history and beliefs of the major religions and denominations of the world in language that is understandable for children. This is a good resource for helping children learn about our contemporary world of faith.

Emotional Intelligence, by Daniel Goleman (New York: Bantam Books, 1995). A major part of our inner (spiritual) lives includes becoming aware of and managing our emotions. Goleman's groundbreaking book provides great insight into our emotions, the ways to work with our emotions, and ways to nurture emotional intelligence in our families.

The Parent's Guide to Protecting Your Children in Cyberspace, by Parry Aftab (New York: McGraw-Hill, 2000). This is an excellent, comprehensive guide to helping parents understand and deal responsibly with the Internet.

Websites

www.beliefnet.com. Very good general website for general religious topics and resources.

www.domestic-church.com. A website primarily for home churching in the Catholic faith.

www.family.org. A Christian-based family website that provides good review information for movies and music (under the "Plugged In" tab).

www.godatthekitchentable.com. My own website that provides resources to help parents teach their religious and moral beliefs to their children.

www.homechurch.com. A website that provides resource and networking opportunities for independent Christians involved in the "house church" movement.

www.homefaith.com. A Catholic-oriented website that provides ideas on sharing faith in the home.

INDEX

ABOUT THE AUTHOR

SCOTT COOPER has several years of experience working with youth, including teaching, coaching, and serving on education and drug-prevention boards. In addition to being the author of *Sticks and Stones*, he has written articles for numerous parenting publications. He is a principal and CFO of an international planning and design firm. He lives with his wife and three children in Northern California.